You Already Made The Decision, You Just Aren't Happy With It

How to Make Better Decisions or Live With the Ones You've Made.

TAMI JAFFE

You Already Made The Decision, You Just Aren't Happy With It

For more information, visit www.tamijaffe.com.

ISBN: 978-1-7357995-0-6

DEDICATION

This book is dedicated to my husband, Dr. Glenn Jaffe, who has been incredibly supportive of my business and me. We may never be able to decide what's for dinner, but I think we have done a pretty fantastic job deciding to live our best lives.

To my daughter Teagan, who is the sweetest and most creative girl and is growing up to be such a loving sister and friend, you always know when mommy needs extra snuggles.

To my daughter, Cora, who knows how to negotiate and ask for what she wants, your energy and sweet spirit keep mommy on her toes.

A SPECIAL BONUS GIFT FROM TAMI

Knowing what the right decision is every time something comes your way can be tough. You may make the decision based on past experience, what you think you want in the moment or because you don't think there's another choice. When you finish this book, you'll be armed with tools to help you make better decisions.

As a special bonus for buying this book, I've created a guide that you can keep on your desk or pull up when you are contemplating a new decision or want to make a lasting change in your life. This Clarity Trifecta Guide will take you through a few key questions you need to ask yourself in order to make the best decision. That way you don't have to pull out the book every time you find yourself faced with a decision that you're not sure how to make.

Just go to www.claritytrifecta.com and let me know where to email your bonus guide.

As another special gift, I'll also be sending tips, tricks, and great information to make your life and business easier.

Let's get started.

TABLE OF CONTENTS

PREFACE

You make thousands of decisions every day with ease and very little thought, yet certain decisions leave you stressed out. You contemplate them for days, weeks, months, and sometimes even years.

You know what I mean, right?

There's something you keep saying you want to do or a change you want to make, but you never seem to be able actually to do it. You might take a few steps in the right direction one day but find yourself falling back into your comfort zone the next day. You seem unable to break through to get what you say you want.

If you find yourself saying you want one thing, but doing another and you're not able to stick to the decisions you say you want, this book is for you.

If you're trying to decide if you should switch careers, start a business, make a change in a relationship, get into a new relationship, move to a new place, improve your health or make any other change that has you procrastinating and leaves you spinning - or just flat out resisting - you're in the right place. This book will give you the steps you need to take to make a better decision and then stick to it.

This book is not going to tell you what the best decision is for you. But it will help you determine how to figure out which decision is best for yourself. Then you can use this process over and over again to continue to make significant decisions and changes in your life.

I am not here to tell you that you need to leave your job or get a divorce or that making any specific change is the right decision. It's up to you to determine what is the best choice for you. I am here to help you gain the tools to help you make those decisions wisely.

When you follow the guidelines laid out for you here, you will be able to make the best decision and accomplish what you've wanted to achieve. You will finally be able to stop procrastinating because you will understand why you were delaying. You will feel confident in your choice instead of allowing indecisiveness to haunt you every day.

If you are 100% satisfied with the state of things in your life and are a master at making decisions, you are probably already implementing what we'll be discussing in this book. If you love your job, are in an incredible relationship, never fight with your children, make all the money you want, are in the best shape of your life, and have no lingering decisions holding you back from having everything you say you want, then you probably don't need to read this book. You may want to pass it on to a friend, a brother or sister, or someone you know that is struggling with their decisions.

But, if you're like most people, you will typically have one or two areas in your life that are going well and then another area that is a struggle. It's the area where you've been struggling that you are typically avoiding or delaying making a decision.

Once you understand the real reason you avoid the decision or don't seem to make progress, you can finally fix it and get what you truly desire.

You may think you've made some mistakes and just can't get this right, but believe me - we've all made mistakes! It's not because you are flawed. It's because the system you have been using to make decisions has been flawed.

The good news is that you don't have to continue doing things the same way. You are in the right place to find the steps you can take to end the cycle of bad decision-making, avoiding decisions, or just not following through once you say you have made a decision.

The process I am sharing with you is one I've developed over a decade. I have combined pieces I've learned from some of the best experts in the world with exercises I have done myself or created for my clients and put them into an easy to follow system. It incorporates all the critical components necessary to make better decisions and stick to them.

I've used this process many times throughout my life to ensure I made the best decision for me and my family, no matter the circumstance. These steps have helped me make some significant transitions as quickly and as seamlessly as possible.

Some of the areas in my life that I've made transitions include: going to seven different schools, strategically changing careers several times, moving to three different states, starting my own business, leaving complicated relationships before it was too late, getting married to the love of my life, having kids I adore, and trying to balance it all while being a leader in my industry. I'm no stranger to making tough decisions and thriving, rather than merely surviving.

I use these same tools to help my clients face challenging decisions now so that they feel empowered to make the right decisions. I am a success coach and consultant who guides my clients through this process, allowing them to make lasting changes seamlessly by making the right decisions.

As you read this book, I encourage you to use a highlighter to highlight the things that stand out to you. Use a pen or pencil to fill in your answers to the questions that I ask you. Make this book your workbook to help you get to the better decision. Yes, I am giving you permission to write in this book! That way, when you open it again, you can see what stood out and exactly what action steps you committed to taking.

The only regret you will ever have about making a better decision is that you didn't make it sooner. So, don't delay any further! Turn this page to get started and make your best decision yet.

CHAPTER 1

Your Decisions Got You Here

"I am not a product of my circumstances. I am a product of my decisions."

—Stephen Covey

Think about where you are in your life right now. Think about every area of your life. Your career or business, how much money you have, your health, weight, marriage, relationship with your kids, and the way you parent. Think about all of it—everything in your life.

Are you happy with it all? Is there anything you want to change?

You may find this surprising, but everything in your life, you decided that's how it would be.

No, really...

These were your decisions. You decided to be exactly where you are right now. Regardless of where any of us are, me included, we decided that this is where we wanted to be.

Would you like for your life to be more than the way it is? Do you wish some things were better?

Of course, you do.

At some point, everybody wakes up and wishes they were getting a better result in their relationships. They want to get along better with their spouse, parents, siblings, friends, boss, or coworkers. They wish they were doing a better job parenting because they don't want to yell, but they did it again just yesterday. So they want to do better today. They look at their money and think I want more money. I'm not satisfied with this. How am I going to pay my bills? How can I take the trip with my family or pay for my kid's college?

Realizing they need to establish all these goals, they make New Year's resolutions and talk to their friends about how they want their lives to be. They wish, they dream, and they create vision boards. They do all this planning, and they still don't get the things they say they want. Sound familiar?

Do you know why they don't get it? The reason why most people rarely achieve what it is they set out to do?

They didn't decide for their goal to happen. You are only at the place in life where you've already decided to be. You will only ever be at the exact spot in your life where you have decided to be.

The fact is, you've made decisions to be precisely where you are. You just don't like the choices you've made.

Hate your life? It was your decision. Love your life? That was your decision. Got a lot of money? Your decision. Broke? Your decision. Unhappy? Your decision. All of it. Your decisions.

People always say, "You've got to make a decision." Every motivational speaker says, "Make a decision." I'm telling you right now, you've made a lot of decisions. What you're living with is the result of all those decisions. You have just made some bad decisions.

You can sit around whining and complaining, but it isn't going to do you any good. Besides, no one wants to hear about it. Your excuses and reasons why you don't have what you want are just another form of your ongoing decision to delay making things better. They are additional bad decisions piled on top of the existing bad decisions.

The good news is you can make better decisions at any time. You always have the opportunity to create a new decision. At any point, you can choose to do something differently. You can decide that enough is enough, and now is the time to turn things around.

If you decide, 'I want more,' that will be your decision.

If you do nothing and continue to live with less, that will be your decision.

You get to decide what you're going to dream about. If it happens, you decided to make it happen. If it doesn't happen, you decided to have a dream that was never going to happen.

There are very few circumstances that I believe are genuinely out of your control.

What we experienced with the Coronavirus, none of us decided to go through. It was out of our control, and it had a significant impact on the world. But we did determine how we would go through it.

Some people sat at home, were miserable, and got depressed and fat. Others took the time to reconnect with their families and enjoy their time together. Some people merely managed the best they could and prayed it wouldn't last long. We each decided how we wanted to go through the pandemic as we all decide how we're going to go through any problem.

Decisions are pretty much the key to everything, more or less. The trouble is, people make countless decisions, then they don't take action on the good ones, and decide to accept and live with the results of the bad ones.

But don't complain about the way it is, because it was your decision for it to be that way.

Sucks, doesn't it?

It's sad, but that's just the reality. You can complain about it. You can whine about it. You can put it on social media. You can take pictures of it. But you must like it because you're putting up with it. Because if you didn't like it, you'd probably make a different decision.

It's as though people don't see the connection between the choices their making and the results they are getting.

It's time to take responsibility and ownership of where you are in life. It's time to stop making excuses and figure out what it is you want. Only then can you start to make better decisions that will help you get there.

If you make better decisions, you could end up living a great life, all as the result of your decisions. If enough of us make better decisions in our lives, we could create a better future, better businesses, better families, and better communities.

So, why is it that so many people make so many bad decisions?

According to the book ***Switch*** by Chip Heath and Dan Heath, the problem is that to make a change, the heart and mind must agree, but frequently the heart and the mind disagree, fervently.

For instance, our rational side wants to lose weight and get in better shape, so it sets the alarm to get up at 5:30 to go for a walk or a run before work. When the alarm goes off, the emotional side wakes up in the dark and wants nothing more than to go back to sleep.

So which side wins? Well, that depends on the decision you make in the moment. But if you can influence both the rational and emotional sides to be in alignment with your choices, it makes it even easier.

Sometimes that takes breaking a habit or a routine and eliminating some unconscious choices you are making every day.

Poor decisions are sometimes based on what you believed at the time. You may not have had all the information or asked the right questions to find out if there was a better decision that could have been made. Knowing what questions to ask, who to ask, and how to apply it are crucial to making the best decisions.

Other times bad decisions are made because it was something we were taught or learned through similar situations to react a certain way but didn't realize that it doesn't apply anymore.

I remember when I started a new job and asked some of the people on my team why they did some procedures a certain way. Their response was "because that's how it has always been done." I heard this so often throughout my career, and it is one of my biggest pet peeves.

If you are doing something a certain way, you should know why. If you don't understand why you should ask:

- Does this make sense?
- Do I need to do it this way?
- Is there a better way to do it?
- What might I be missing by doing it this way?

Almost always, when we would start digging into a process, we'd figure out that there was a better way to do it or that the reason someone did it a certain way before didn't apply anymore. Like the time they told me, they had to make a report in an exact format for another team because that's how it was always sent it to them, and it needed to be that way. But when we reached out to the other side and asked a few simple questions, we found out that they didn't even need the report anymore because they could get all the information directly from the application.

The same is true with your decisions and how you systematically do certain things. You need to take the time to stop and question yourself:

- Why do I do it that way?
- What is the benefit?
- Is it essential?
- Is it getting you closer to your bigger desires?

It might be time to let go of some of those old decisions that are holding you back.

Most of us have problems because we fool ourselves into believing something that isn't completely true or thinking we need something we don't.

Millions of people struggle to reach their goals and feel like there is a glass ceiling holding them down from achieving what they want and waiting for it to be removed or shattered.

The good news is that your goals are within your reach, and you are not flawed just because you haven't reached them yet. You just haven't been equipped with the right tools to help you reach those goals.

I want you to think about the first question I asked you in this chapter about your life, what you have, and if you were happy with it. Write down a decision or change for each area below you want or need to make that you will be focused on as you read this book.

Career or Business: Examples include changing jobs, hiring someone, firing someone, starting a business you've been thinking about, adding something new or eliminating something in your business or getting educated in a new area to expand your skillsets.

____

____

____

____

Relationships: Examples include deciding to mend a broken relationship with someone, leaving an abusive relationship, getting into a romantic relationship, getting married, accepting and loving yourself, or improving your parenting skills.

____

____

Health: Examples include losing weight, starting to exercise, giving up an unhealthy habit, or dealing with a chronic health issue or pain.

Finances/Income: Examples include paying off debt, finding another source of income, stop spending more than you make, or saving for a vacation, kids college or retirement.

Other: Is there another area of your life that you want to make a decision? It could be something to do with your lifestyle, where you live, something you want to do.

CHAPTER 2

Do You Really Want to Decide

> *"You can complain about the direction of your life all you want, but until you sit in the driver's seat and begin to drive yourself, you aren't going to get where you want to go!"*
>
> —Les Brown

I get done with work for the day, go into my husband's office for a chiropractic adjustment, and as I'm about to walk out the door, he says, "What do you want for dinner?"

I respond, "What do we have?" As I roll my eyes and think, why are you asking me? You're the one who bought groceries, what did you plan to make? By the end of the day, the last thing I want to think about is going home and preparing food. I'd much rather grab something on the way home.

My husband enjoys cooking and does it superbly. Whereas I can cook, but I don't enjoy it much. He likes going to the grocery store, but apparently, he doesn't like planning what we are going to eat because this is a conversation we have almost every night.

It's exhausting! I think we are each wishing the other would just make the decision!

Avoiding the Decision

> *"You cannot afford to live in potential for the rest of your life; at some point, you have to unleash the potential and make your move."*
>
> —Eric Thomas

There are times when you do everything you can to avoid making the decision. You become paralyzed by it and so afraid that you decide it's better not to make a decision. Other times you say you want something, but every action you take shows that you are doing the exact opposite.

What is this telling you?

You may be avoiding the decision because you want to make the perfect decision or have things go exactly the way you want. So until you can figure out how to make that happen, you don't make any decision. But you don't always have to make the perfect decision. You just need to continue making better and better decisions. Each decision is starting to make progress in the right direction.

When you try to avoid making a decision, you are trying to avoid life. You might be trying to avoid a significant change that will come with the decision or afraid of how it will impact others around you. But you can't avoid life. It will go on with or without you agreeing to it, so why not make a decision that gets you closer to where you want to be. Then take one step at a time to adjust and move forward.

Indecision is not a decision! "Maybe" is not a decision! These are just another way of not making a clear decision or putting it off. If you want to make progress, you have to decide one way or the other.

Indecision is a form of self-abuse. You are not trusting yourself to make a decision one way or the other. When you linger in the uncertainty, you are creating more and more stress and anxiety.

Just decide something and start moving forward. You can always adjust your decision later. People who are faster at making decisions go further faster, and it isn't always because they made the best decisions. It's because they made a decision, decided to move forward, and then adjusted their choices based on the results they got several times before other people have even made a decision or taken the first step.

If you don't know what the better decision is yet, first try saying no to something that isn't working for you. Identifying something that isn't working will open up some space for something better to fill the space.

Avoiding a decision is making a decision. You are deciding that you don't want it right now. You are saying you need more information to make a better decision, or you're not ready to implement a change.

To stop avoiding decisions, you have to get clear on why you truly want something and what it will take for you to get it—more on this in chapter 6.

When You're Forced to Make a Decision

"You're going to go through tough times – that's life. But I say, 'Nothing happens to you, it happens for you.' see the positive in negative events."

—Joel Osteen

You can choose to make a change, or sometimes you become stubborn or set in your ways, and it takes someone else pushing you off the ledge for you to change. Sometimes we are forced to make a change like getting fired or having someone leave you.

When people get fired, most of the time, it's from a job they didn't like to begin with, or they were working for someone they didn't trust.

Many times, the person has been thinking about doing something different but didn't have the guts to step out and make it happen.

Sometimes it's God, the universe, fate, or whatever you want to call it telling us it's time. Stop acting like you didn't want it to happen or hadn't been thinking about it.

Just like when someone else physically pushes you, you sometimes get bruised or a little scratch. It might slow you down a little, but you get back up and start going again. Other times when you get pushed, you fall hard and break a leg or two and find yourself paralyzed for a while. You may even get stuck in the blame and anger game and get so caught up in being mad at the person who did it to you that you can't even think of another option. You might also get depressed, anxious, or even freak out.

If you find yourself in a circumstance where you are being forced to make a change, give yourself a minute to absorb what has happened. If you need a day to vent, pout and cry, then take it. But then you need to get up and figure out a way to move on.

The longer you stay in that place of anger, frustration, and blame, the more you give that other person or situation control over you. They are the ones winning when you can't seem to move forward. You cannot control their decisions or their reasons for deciding to let you go or leave you, but you can control how you handle it. You can control what you do next, how you move forward, and whether you will become stronger or weaker because of it.

I met an old colleague at a coffee shop one day just to catch up and see how things were going. He mentioned a lot of changes that were happening and said he wasn't sure how much longer he'd be with the company, but he also didn't think his job was in immediate jeopardy.

A couple of months later, he reached out and asked to set up a consult with me because he wanted to start looking at his career options. The day before we were supposed to meet, he sent me a message that he was just let go from his job.

He wanted to reschedule our appointment as his mind was still swirling from what he had just been told. A few days later, we sat down and started talking about what had happened. He shared that he was outraged and hurt at first, which is understandable after spending years at a company just to be let go with no warning or real reason.

I said to him, "You must have wanted a change because that is why you set up a time to talk to me in the first place. Do you think this could be a good thing for you?"

He had to stop and think about that for a while. It's hard to see the light sometimes when you're in the middle of the darkness of the situation. Once he stopped and thought about it, he said, "you know, there are several things I would like to do, but I just didn't have the time and wasn't sure how to get started on them."

His initial reaction was to go out and find another job to have some security. But the more we talked about what he wanted out of his life, what he enjoyed doing, and how he wanted to live, it became apparent that he was meant to start the business he had been thinking about for years.

After just a few sessions in working together, his confidence level had changed entirely. He was excited about his business, doing all the right things to get started, and was completely clear on the direction he was going.

But before he could get there, he had to realize this didn't happen to him; this happened for him. This situation allowed him to do something new, start his own business, and use his unique skills to serve his clients. Let me repeat that because this is big, it didn't happen *to* him; it happened *for* him.

When you have these circumstances happen to you that you feel are the end of the world and will take you years to recover from, think about it from all angles and consider what positive might come out of it. Consider what role you may have played that led to that situation, whether consciously or subconsciously. Sometimes you create conditions for yourself that will lead to a better future, but in the moment, you feel like everything is collapsing around you.

In these moments, don't let the lesson you are meant to learn go to waste. You can make a better future for yourself if you choose. Decide what you want next and work towards that instead of lingering in the feelings of the past.

If you lost your job, write down all the things you liked and all the things you didn't like about it. Make a list of what you want out of your next job or business and the things you don't want.

You can do the same thing if you went through a breakup, had someone quit, or lost a client. Getting clear on what you want will help you focus on the future and the best options for you. Knowing what you don't want can be just as powerful as knowing what you do want.

Excuses and Justifications

> *"In life, you can have an excuse, or you can have an obstacle that is an opportunity to learn and to grow. Observe your thoughts and throw away your excuses!"*
>
> —Dean Graziosi

Most people have justified why they can't do more, be more, or get more in their lives. It's typically something around family, stress, time, or money. There is an underlying fear under each of these that they are using as an excuse.

Those that want something badly enough will find a way to make it happen.

What are the excuses and justifications that you are telling yourself? Fill in the blank:

If it weren't for ____________________, *I could be doing what I really want to do.*

I've probably heard all excuses and even used most of them. It's easy to blame it on something or someone else when things aren't going your way. Explanations are just ways of saying you haven't committed to it, chosen it, or haven't made it a priority.

Time is a common excuse for people not to start something or do something that they keep saying they want to do. The truth is that you have chosen to make other things a priority.

If you find yourself saying "I don't have the time" a lot, then try taking the No Time Complaining Challenge. This is agreeing not to complain about time in any form. So, not making excuses with your kids that you don't have time to do that with them right now and not telling your spouse your too busy to have a conversation with them.

Instead, look at what is more important to you at the moment and be honest about it. This isn't always easy, but it will make a massive shift in how you look at your time and where your priorities lie. You'll also realize that you've been making a lot of time excuses!

Try blocking out your time for things on the calendar, even stuff like playtime with the kids. When they know they have 30 minutes with you at 6:30, and you are entirely focused on them and not distracted by other things, they will get more value out of that time.

If you've been putting off a project because you don't have the time, take a look at your calendar right now and see when it makes sense to schedule it. Then stick to it!

If time is one of your primary excuses then you may need to look at where you are spending your time and figure out what can be eliminated if you want to add something new in.

When it comes to money as an excuse, it typically doesn't have anything to do with money. There is always something more profound. You don't want it bad enough, or you aren't willing to give up something else in order to get it.

You may be living out the excuses your parents always made around money or a money story you've been letting hold you back. When you can identify what these are, only then can you finally start letting them go. Recognize when you are using them and ask yourself if it is true for you now.

I was shopping with my kids, and my daughter was asking for a toy, and I heard myself say to her, "Is it on sale?" As I heard myself say it, I cringed. I heard the same thing from my mom growing up all the time. We weren't allowed to buy clothes or toys or anything unless it was on sale. I had developed this money story that I shouldn't buy things unless they were on sale or a good deal.

It wasn't even that we couldn't afford what she was asking. She even had her own money from birthday gifts. It was just a natural reaction, and the underlying message to my daughter was that you aren't worth it unless it's cheap.

We all carry different money baggage with us, and until we stop using it as an excuse and know where we stand with our money, we will never make any progress.

When you use family or someone else as an excuse for why you can't make a decision or a change, you are giving that person control over your situation. Now I'm not saying you should never consider anyone else's feelings or how your decision will impact someone else. Of course, you need to consider these things, but you need to know when it is an excuse or a legitimate reason.

Here are some common family justifications I hear a lot that are usually just an excuse. There's a more significant underlying fear that is keeping the person from doing it now.

- My spouse would never let me do that.
- I have to wait until my kids are out of the house.
- My kids' schedule is too crazy.
- My family is my top priority, and I can't do something for myself.
- I'm worried about what my parents would say.

The flip side of the family issues is that you might be avoiding taking any responsibility. You believe that what is happening is out of your control or isn't your problem or fault. When a child is on drugs, the issue doesn't get fully resolved until each parent and the child all take full ownership of the situation. They have to admit that this is their problem and commit to solving it.

The same is true in relationships. Both people have to take one hundred percent ownership of the problem and commit to resolving it for there to be complete reconciliation. The blame and excuses have to stop, and each person has to own their part and commit to resolving the issue to move forward.

What are some of the excuses and justifications that you are making? Where are you not taking complete ownership of an issue? Admitting to them is the first step to being able to stop using them as excuses and moving forward.

Write down the excuses and justifications that you find yourself saying now.

____

____

____

____

What is one step you can take to stop using these as an excuse or justification?

____

____

____

____

What Are You Getting From The Way It Is Now

> *"We are products of our past, but we don't have to be prisoners of it."*
>
> —Rick Warren

There is something you are getting out of the situation. It's filling you up in some way. What are you getting out of it? A lot of times, it is fear that keeps you from moving on or resistant to change. But the reality is, you're also getting something from the current situation.

Whether it's giving you comfort from eating food that isn't healthy for you, it satisfies you at that moment and keeps you from losing the weight you want to lose. Or it's the passion or adrenaline you get after getting in a fight and then going through the reconciliation. Maybe you like the energy that comes from being able to have an awkward conversation with somebody. It brings a release to be able to say what you believe and a feeling of liberating to be able to say what you feel, but you're not paying attention to how you are saying it or its impact on someone else. There are so many ways that we can fill ourselves up with things that aren't helping us.

To make a change, you have got to find the other ways to fill yourself up. You've got to find another way to get the energy source that you're getting from that situation.

It's tough just to quit cold turkey; any program will tell you this. If you're trying to cut out caffeine, it's best to wean yourself off slowly. If you're trying to cut sugar, you will stick to it better if you can replace it with something else in the beginning.

If you desire to leave your job and start a business, you have to look at what that job provides for you. Is it providing you the security and the financial well-being that you need? Does it satisfy a need to be around people? Starting a business can feel isolating at times. Is it playing to your need for acknowledgment from others?

You are getting something out of it, or you would have left by now. When you figure out what it is, you can find ways to meet that need in more fulfilling and beneficial ways.

If it's financial security, you need to develop a financial plan that will make you feel secure. That may mean working while you start a business or knowing you have enough in your savings to sustain you for the period it will take to your business to get to a profitable point.

If you love the social aspect of your job, you need to find networking groups and maybe get into a collaborative space to fill that need while building your business.

•

Do you see how some of these needs may be holding you back from actually making a change that you say you want? Know that you have other options to help fulfill some of those same needs. Many times they are much healthier options and will benefit you more than what is giving you the fulfillment today.

Some of the ways you find to replace that need will be temporary solutions, like getting a job while you build your business, or running a mile before you run a marathon. Those interim steps are critical because you don't jump from point A to Z without going through B, C, D, and so on. You have to take each step one at a time. So, to let go of the thing that you're saying you don't want, and get what you do want, you may have to find that interim fulfillment.

My kids have a book called ***Have You Filled A Bucket Today*** by Carol McCloud, and it teaches kids how we all carry around these invisible buckets and how to fill up other people's buckets. The bucket's purpose is to hold your kind thoughts and feelings about yourself. The book emphasizes how by filling up other people's buckets and doing helpful things for others, it also helps fill up your bucket. It describes how there are ways that you can also take from other people's buckets by not being kind.

We all have these invisible buckets with different needs in them that we want to be fulfilled. Think about the area of your life where you are feeling stuck and want to move forward or make a change. What is it satisfying for you? What are you getting out of it that you may not have even realized before? What energy sources may you be getting from it? What is the benefit of not changing it or moving forward? What are you getting from this situation that, in some way, is giving you something that you need? What are you getting out of that relationship? Out of eating unhealthy or being in a job that isn't fulfilling to you? From spending more than you make or fill in the blank with your current struggle? What are some of the things that you're getting from a positive standpoint?

____

____

____

____

It might surprise you what comes up when you stop and think about it from this different perspective. But to actually make the change and move forward, you also need to determine other ways to fulfill that same need when it is a healthy need or ways to eliminate the need when it is unhealthy and not serving you.

You may find yourself staying in the relationship because there is no other source for you to receive that love; there's no other source for you to fill that part of your bucket. Sometimes that source needs to come from yourself. Sometimes you need to be the one to show yourself self-love, show yourself self-respect, and show yourself self-discipline.

When you can do that, you will feel full. You will already be fulfilled, and not depending on someone else or something else to fill you up. You're not reaching for the relationship that you know will hurt you in the long run because you found the love that you have in yourself, which is now stronger than the love that anyone else can give you. You won't be reaching for that piece of cake when you really should be reaching for that apple, because you already have the fulfillment that you needed.

Take 5 minutes now to think about ways to fill the need that your current situation is fulfilling for you. How can you find other sources to fill those same needs?

___

___

___

___

CHAPTER 3

Stop Ignoring The Signs

"The signs are there telling you it is time for a change, stop ignoring them."

—Tami Jaffe

Life is complicated! We think we have things all figured out and know exactly what we want, and then we are thrown a curveball. Many signs happen to us, around us, or within us, trying to tell us that it is time for a change. When you can recognize and listen to the signs, then you can make decisions and changes much faster.

Suppose you ignore the signs or don't even realize that flags are waving at you to do something differently. In that case, you can get stuck in a job, a relationship, or another situation that leaves you unfulfilled, stressed, or feeling like you've settled. The longer you ignore the signs, the worse it gets, and the more it has an impact on your emotions, your health, and your ability to move forward and move on. To help you recognize the signs and stop ignoring them, we will discuss the signs that may be showing up in your life and what they may be trying to tell you.

You're Feeling Blah

When you start to feel a little flat, you don't care about things like you used to, and nothing excites you anymore, it is a sign that something needs to change. You might think you only need to make a significant change when you are to the point of being depressed, but feeling unsatisfied and bored are the first signs that show up before getting to the point of depression. This comes from no longer being excited about what you do. It's like you've lost your inspiration.

When you start to feel like there is no drive, do some self-reflection to determine if it's just a bad day or if there is something beneath the surface. Think about the area you feel indifferent to and discover why it no longer interests you. What used to make you happy and excited about that area, and what has changed?

You Feel Stuck

When you feel like you can't get out of a situation and there seems to be no other choice, it's time to evaluate what's going on. Many times when you're feeling stuck, you start dreaming about how things could be, and you're not content with where they are. You have no idea how you go from being stuck to making strides towards the things that bring you joy.

If you find yourself feeling this way or telling people that you are stuck in a job, a relationship, or another area of your life, you need to start asking yourself what needs to change. As soon as you know what's bothering you, then you need to take action.

Suzanne Evans, the Founder of Driven, Inc., always says, *"If you keep saying you're stuck, replace the word stuck with stubborn."* Most of the time, you're not stuck, you're just stubborn. You don't want to make the decision or do the hard work it takes to make things better.

Life is going to move on, and you can either move forward or find yourself in the same situation next year. Choose to take a step to get out of the mud in which you find yourself stuck.

You Sense You're Settling

Good is not always good enough. You're settling when you start questioning if you deserve more, asking is this it, or you just have that gut feeling that things aren't quite right. You will never know if there is something better out there waiting for you unless you explore the options.

If it's your job that you are settling for, then look at what would interest you more. What could you be doing every day to make yourself feel more challenged, teach you more, and make you happier?

If you feel like you are settling in your relationship, you may need to try new things with your partner. If you're not being treated well and your partner doesn't respect you, you need to figure out why you would be with someone who doesn't recognize who you are. Often, the way we get treated is a reflection on us, and we first have to change who we are before we see any change in our relationships.

Identify where you're settling and ask yourself what needs to change.

Your Energy is Low

Do you wake up feeling drained before the day has even started? Have you been avoiding doing anything more than the bare minimum and started telling your friends that you can't hang out? If your energy is low and there's no underlying health reason for it, you may just be exhausted from spending so much time on things that don't matter to you.

It's time to look at everything you're doing and figure out what is draining you and cut it out of your life. Then look at what things light you up that you need to be doing more. Think about the last time you felt invigorated and alive. What were you doing? Maybe you need to be doing more of that.

Your Environment Has Become Toxic

All jobs and all relationships have some level of stress. It's when the times of stress outweigh the times of enjoyment that it starts to become toxic. When the thought of going to work or having to talk to someone makes you depressed and physically ill, it's gone too far. It starts impacting other areas of your life, and it can feel like there is no escaping it.

Ask yourself these questions as a check-in to see if you are showing signs of being in a toxic environment:

- How are you sleeping? Are you able to fall right to sleep, sleep through the night and wake up feeling refreshed? Or do you wake up in the middle of the night worrying about your situation and what to do?
- How are your eating habits? Do you stress eat everything in sight or starve yourself because you feel too sick to eat?
- Are you feeling safe at home and work?

If you are struggling with these, then it is time to start looking at how you can change things for the better or start building your exit strategy to get out of the toxic environment.

You're Coping in an Unhealthy Way

There are times when a glass of wine or a piece of cake helps you relax and unwind. However, when you find yourself drinking the entire bottle (night after night) and not just stopping at one piece of cake but eating the cake and the cookies and still wanting more, then you are just searching for a way to cope and find comfort. It might start as just a way to relax or find peace, but when it becomes a habit, it's time to make a change before it becomes an addiction.

These unhealthy habits can come in many different forms like alcohol, drugs, food, binge-watching Netflix, and shopping, just to name a few. Whatever your poison might be, you are trying to block out discomfort and stress by pouring something into your life that makes you feel better in the moment or numbs the feelings.

Instead of addressing the real issue head-on, you're turning to these unhealthy habits. If you don't look at making a change now, the next thing you know a year will have passed by, and it's only gotten worse.

Start now by taking a look at what is happening when you feel the need to pour that glass of wine, eat the dessert, or watch an entire season in one day. What are you trying to drown out, avoid, or put off as long as you can? When you can identify what the trigger is, you can start looking at what needs to change in that area of your life.

Your Body is Giving You Signs

Do you feel chronic pain in an area of your body? Have you been diagnosed with a disease? There is a reason that they are called diseases. Break it apart, and it is dis-ease. Our mind is not at ease, and our body is a reflection of that. Marianne Williamson says, "It's not the body that gets sick, but the mind."

I have torn my ACL twice in my life and have had four knee surgeries. Years later, I found out that knee injuries are a sign of being afraid of moving forward. When I looked back at the time they happened, I could see why.

The first time, I was a junior in high school, and my parents had just told me that they wanted me to switch from the private school I was into the public school for my senior year. It would be the 3rd high school I had been to and leaving my friends my senior year and going to a school where I didn't know anyone was scary. I'd have to give up playing sports for half of the year and miss out on the senior trip with my friends. It was not how I had envisioned my senior year.

The second time, I had just gotten out of a seven-year relationship after finding out that he had been cheating. Both of these situations brought a fear of moving forward with my life.

Each area of our body is a signal for what is going on in our minds. When we don't deal with the fears, anger, frustrations, resentment, and other emotions, our bodies will develop chronic pain, disease, or we have injuries that cause us to slow down. If you try to avoid the feelings, it will continue to get worse. I'm not going to go into great detail on this in this book, but if you want to learn more about this, you can read *Heal Your Body* by Louise Hay.

Whatever the sign is that you are getting, you first have to recognize that it is even a sign. See that these are signs waving at you that it is time to make a change. If you keep ignoring them, things get worse and worse, and you end up having to decide out of sheer desperation, and by then, you don't have the best options.

Some of these signs might be your wakeup call. The moment that you realize that something has to change. The incident that makes you stop and think about your life in a whole new way. We'll talk more about your wakeup call in Chapter 10 and how that can be the moment that drives your commitment to making a change.

As you read through these signs, did any of them resonate with you? Did you read one and think, oh shoot, that's where I am? Did any of them make you feel uneasy? I want you to write down the signs that have been waving at you in your life. Why have you been ignoring them? Or what have you done to acknowledge them so that you can make a decision to help you move forward?

____

____

____

____

CHAPTER 4

Make the Decision!

"In any moment of decision, the best thing you can do is the right thing, the next best thing is the wrong thing, and the worst thing you can do is nothing."

—Theodore Roosevelt

All decisions are not equal. We embrace some decisions, like marriages, babies, new homes, or a new job. But then other decisions we resist with everything in us. We don't even think about some decisions; we make them with no effort and little thought. Other decisions we are contemplating for days, weeks, months, and sometimes even years.

Decision-making is a muscle that must be exercised. For some people making quick decisions come more natural while others are more reflective and take longer to make decisions. Some like to have all the data and know the consequences of each decision before committing to one while others go with their intuition with very little information.

For this discussion, let's call these two types of decision-makers the "Quick" decision-makers and the "Slow" decision-makers. Both types of people can apply different skills to improve their decision-making ability.

The Quick decision-maker typically goes with their gut or a trained instinct that helps them see a situation and quickly determine their preference. The benefits of the Quick decision makers are:

- They get quick results and can see what is working and what isn't working.
- They typically adjust when they see what isn't working as planned and make a new decision.
- They tend to get farther faster just because of their ability to decide quickly and adjust quickly.

What gets in the way for the Quick decision-makers is when the ego gets involved. They can jump to conclusions too quickly or not be willing to adjust to prove a point. When the decision doesn't help them get to the bigger goal but instead just plays to their ego to make them feel like they accomplished something or want to prove something, they can get caught in the trap of making poor decisions that they end up regretting.

If you are in the Quick decision-making group, here are some things you can do to help you make better decisions:

- Ask some questions before deciding to evaluate all your options.
- Understand how this decision will impact your long term goal.
- Be willing to recognize when you were wrong and make a new decision.

Slow decision makers will typically take their time to reflect on their options. The benefits of the Slow decision makers are:

- They ask questions to get more information.
- They gather data and try to make an informed decision.
- They weigh the options before moving forward.

The Slow decision-maker's downfall is that they can take so long to decide that the opportunity passes them by or someone else makes the decision for them. They can also get caught up in analysis paralysis where they don't progress in moving forward because they are too busy analyzing everything. Even decisions that should be easy become complicated, and they over-analyze. They can also fall into perfectionism paralysis and not decide because they're afraid their choice is not perfect, and they don't realize that they can always change it later.

If you fall into the Slow decision-maker category, here are some things you can do to help you make better decisions:

- Learn how to make quicker decisions and use your intuition more.
- Find a balance to know what decisions require thoughtful analysis and contemplation versus those that can be made with ease and speed.

In this chapter, I am giving you a few tools that you can use to make quicker decisions or quick questions you can ask yourself that will put your choices into a new perspective so that you can get to a better decision faster.

These tools are great for helping you make the initial decision, but so many choices you make require a lasting change. A change that you have to recommit to almost every day, or you will fall back into your comfort zone or not take the right steps to keep moving forward. Decisions that impact you for days, months, and even years will require focus every day to make them successful. Decisions such as deciding to lose weight, starting a business, changing careers, leaving an unfulfilling relationship, or dealing with a health issue.

For those types of changes, you will need to consistently make decisions every day to have a lasting change. In the chapters following this, I will present the formula to make those lasting changes.

Quick Decision Training

> *"Your success in life isn't based on your ability to simply change. It is based on your ability to change faster than your competition, customers, and business."*
>
> —Mark Sanborn

What should I wear today? Where should I go for lunch? What should I order? How should I respond to that email? Sometimes even the littlest decisions take us too long to make. If you want to develop your decision-making skills, it takes practice. There are some tools that you can use to exercise your brain's ability to make quicker decisions.

Try making quick decisions for things that don't matter. Like what's your favorite color or animal. You can always change it tomorrow. But for today, pick one.

For little things throughout the day that you know you need to do, just say 3-2-1 Go! Then take action and do it. When your alarm goes off, say 3-2-1 Go and get up for the day. Don't linger in bed or think about hitting your snooze button. When you find yourself delaying doing something, try to put yourself into quick action and decide to start.

Nothing forces a decision faster than a deadline! Try setting a timer and only giving yourself a specific amount of time to make a decision. If you usually take ten minutes to decide what you are going to wear in the morning, cut it in half and give yourself five minutes. After a few days, cut the timer back by another minute and then a few days later another minute. Setting a time forces you to stay in the moment and get your decision made quickly and effectively.

For some substantial decisions, you may need to give yourself a day or a week. But put a deadline on it and do not let yourself go beyond that time. Remember that any decision is better than no choice.

The more you practice being more decisive with even small decisions, the more your memory muscle grows, and you can make bigger decisions more quickly as well.

Being in a place of indecision is self-abuse. It takes a ton of energy and drains you to be in that place of indecision for too long. It's time to commit to making the decision quicker to move forward.

Write down three decisions you need to make and set a timeframe for making the decision. How are you going to make that decision faster and more decisively?

1. ____

Date: ________________________

2. ____

Date: ________________________

3. ____

Date: ________________________

The Miracle Question

"It's not the strongest or most intelligent who will survive but those who can best manage change."

—Charles Darwin

In Solution Focused Therapy, they use a line of questioning that has you think about the future to find solutions. One of the tools used in some difficult situations where the person cannot see another option, understand how things could be different, or find a solution, is called the "Miracle Question."

The Miracle Question is framed like this; After you put down this book and finish up your day, you go to sleep tonight and sleep well. In the middle of the night, a miracle happens, and all your problems are solved. When you wake up, you don't know yet what has happened. As you get up, what is the first small sign that would make you wonder; did a miracle happen? The problem is gone! How would you discover that this miracle occurred? What is different?

By taking this approach, you should be able to identify tangible things that would be different in your life if you made a change. You can start to see how you could live your life without the obstacles in your way, without the excuses and justifications and without the blurred lens through which you see things right now.

When you can picture your life without the current problem, envision how you would wake up differently, and go throughout your day in a new way, you can start doing some of those things even before the problem is gone. You can change the pattern that got you into this place.

If you are usually snapping at your kids in the morning to get ready and to be responsible, how would that be different if the problems didn't exist? You'd probably wake up, smile at them, give them a big hug, and tell them how much you love them. This gesture would change how they respond to you. Instead of fighting you each morning, they will be more cooperative.

Even though your problem may not be completely gone, you can start doing these things now. Making a small shift like how you talk to your family in the morning will start your day off with a ripple effect that impacts everyone in your house. Your stress levels go down, and so does everyone else's. Then you can start to have meaningful conversations to solve the problems instead of brushing them under the rug and pretending they don't exist.

The same is true for other types of problems. Start by looking at what things in your life would be different and how things would feel different. Identify the tangible things that will tell you that you've had a miracle happen.

Do this exercise now and write down the first thing you would notice if your problems were gone. Picture yourself waking up tomorrow morning and a miracle occurred overnight. What is the first sign you have that something is different? How would you know that a miracle occurred?

____

____

____

____

____

What would you do differently this day that you didn't do today?

____

____

____

____

____

The Rocking Chair Test

> *"Twenty years from now you will be more disappointed by the things that you didn't do than by the ones you did do. So throw off the bowlines. Sail away from the safe harbor. Catch the trade winds in your sails. Explore. Dream. Discover."*
>
> —Mark Twain

A friend of mine told me about her grandmother and how she would always ask her to apply the rocking chair test when trying to make a big decision. Her grandmother would say, "Darling, when you are older and sitting on your front porch in your rocking chair, and you look back at what you decided to do, will you be proud of your decision? Will you be satisfied of the steps that you took to get where you are? Will you be proud of how you handled the situation? If you can say yes, then you are making the right decision."

We can get lost in the moment and all the pressures around us. By thinking about sitting in that rocking chair on your front porch in 10, 20, or even 30 years from now, telling your grandkids what you did and the decisions you made, you will take yourself out of the pressures of the moment and make a better decision for your future.

Suzy Welch invented a simple tool called the 10/10/10 to help people make decisions and move forward. With this approach, you think about the decisions you make on three different time frames: How will you feel about it 10 minutes, ten months, and ten years from now?

This tool is similar to the rocking chair method in that it helps us see things with a fresh perspective. It helps to make sure that regret is not part of our life. If you can foresee that a decision you make now is likely to leave you with regret later, it means that you need to rethink your decision and find another path to choose so that you can have a happier future.

As you think about the specific decision you are faced with right now, think about yourself sitting on that rocking chair in 10 years and looking back. How do you feel about the decision you made?

You have to ask yourself this from both sides of the equation. If you chose to make a change versus stay in a situation. If you decided to start something new versus put it off another 5-10 years. Whatever the two sides of the decision you face. You may confront more than two options, but typically there will be two choices that stand out as the best options in your mind. If you have more choices, you can do this for the additional options as well.

Take a few minutes right now to just picture yourself ten years in the future. How do you feel about the decision you've made? Write out for both options what you think at that moment, telling your kids, grandkids, or friends about the choice you faced and what it has done for you over the past ten years.

Decision A Reflection:

____

____

____

____

Decision B Reflection:

____

____

____

____

CHAPTER 5

The Formula For Lasting Change

"The first step to getting somewhere is to decide that you are not going to stay where you are."

—JP Morgan

When you're not completely clear on what you want, there is no way that you can bring it to fruition. There is no way that you're ever going to make a plan that will help you get you there when you don't know exactly where "there" is.

When you get clear on what you want and why you want it, things can start to become a reality. Only then will things begin to transform for you. It will give you the drive and the motivation to stay on course and take the steps you need to make a change.

Gaining clarity brings you certainty, which helps to build your confidence in your ability to do it. To make a lasting change, you need to feel confident in your decision and believe in yourself.

Clarity also helps to grow your courage. If you understand not just what you want and why you want it, but also how you could make it happen and what steps you need to take to make it happen, then your courage starts to grow. You develop the courage to take that first step. And as you take that first step, your courage grows even more, and you can take that second step, and then you can take the third step. It's a progression.

It's not like you just wake up one day, and all of a sudden, dare to change everything all at once. You have to take small steps one at a time. And there may be setbacks along the way, but when you have clarity, it will help get you back on track.

The third piece that clarity helps develop is your commitment. Now that you know what you want and why you want it now, you're committed to it.

I call this the "Clarity Trifecta."

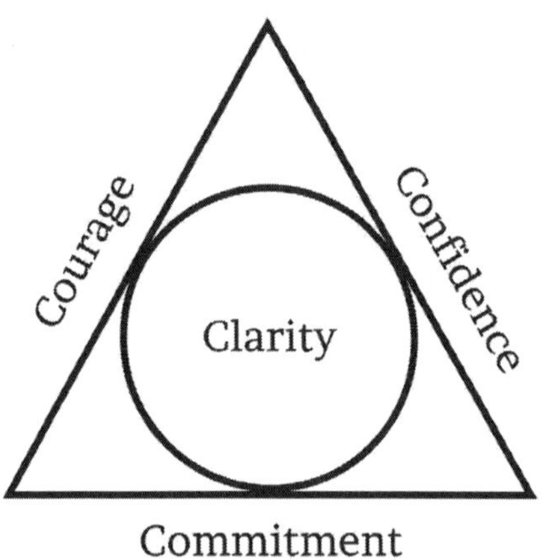

When you are first starting to make a change, your Clarity Trifecta starts out really small.

Clarity helps you know what you want, why you want it, and how you can make it happen. Then as you get more precise, the clarity bubble in the middle expands. And as that expands, it starts to stretch out and grow your confidence, courage, and commitment.

However, the three sides of the triangle don't expand proportionately. Your commitment might start to grow first when you are clear on the change you want to make. Then you begin to gain some confidence that you can make this happen. As you start to take steps and see how the change is really possible, your courage grows. You may find that one side grows faster for you than the others. The other two sides have to catch up as you move forward to create your lasting change.

Consistency circles the entire Clarity Trifecta because a triangle cannot roll and build momentum on its own.

To get the snowball effect, you have to be consistent. Be consistent in looking for more and more clarity, develop your confidence, dare to take each step, and be utterly committed to the change you want. Consistency is what creates the momentum that will make the transition more comfortable and easier as you go.

When I first decided that I wanted to leave my corporate job, I had to go through a process. At first, I wasn't sure exactly what I wanted to do, so I sought a coach to help me figure it out. Here are some of the areas of clarity that I needed to determine:

- What was the actual business going to be?
- What services would I offer?

- Who were my ideal clients?
- How was I going to get my message out to the right people?
- What was my marketing message?
- What sets me apart from competitors?
- What training did I need?

The list goes on, but I think you get the point. As I started filling in the information and getting more explicit, I began to see how it was possible. As the clarity grows, it expands the Clarity Trifecta, and the other sides of the triangle will begin to grow.

Having clarity around my business started developing my confidence to attract the right clients. By getting clear on my plan, I got the courage to take those first steps. My commitment grew when I was clear on why I wanted this and what it would mean to achieve it.

As I continued working on my message and hearing people's feedback, it continued to bring me more clarity. I got more confident about how to communicate my message. My courage grew as I served more people and saw the results that my clients were getting. My commitment grew as I got closer and closer to my goal of leaving my job and being my own boss.

Then as all these areas expanded, my momentum started to build, and by remaining consistent, I was able to create a lasting change.

You can see how this works with this example of starting a business. The same formula works for a change in a relationship you want to make or losing weight or any change that you wish to make.

I will go into more detail on each of these five areas in the following chapters and give you some tools to apply to help you grow each one.

CHAPTER 6

Clarity

"A lack of clarity could put the brakes on any journey to success."

—Steve Maraboli

If you're resisting a change, it is usually due to a lack of clarity. You are not clear on precisely what you want, why you want it, how you could get it, or what it will look like when you get it.

No wonder you are resisting!

When you can get clear on these specifics, you will find a way to get what you want.

First, you want to understand what the problem is and why you want to change it. But understanding the problem alone doesn't automatically solve it. In this chapter, we will be going over the different pieces of clarity you need to get to help you make the right decision.

Understanding why you want to make a change will help drive you forward. If you know why you don't want to stay where you are, it enables you to see why you want to make this decision to do something different.

The Good, The Bad and The Ugly

"Any change, even a change for the better, is always accompanied by drawbacks and discomforts."

—Arnold Bennett

There are always multiple layers to any given situation. Depending on the type of person you are, you probably tend to focus more on either the good or the bad. If you're the glass half full person, you are focused on the good and the positives happening. If you're the glass-half-empty person, you focus more on the bad and negative things happening.

Before you make your decision, I want you to think about all the components of the area of your life in which you want to make a change. To help open your eyes to some things you may have overlooked and give you more clarity on your existing situations, let's take a look at the good, the bad, and the ugly.

I always like to start with the good because too many times it gets overlooked. When you are in the midst of a situation causing stress, it can be challenging to see any positive in the situation.

Think about the area in your life that you want to decide to make a change and ask yourself, what is good about it? What has been going well for you in your career, business, relationships, finances, health, or some other area of your life? Just because you might be ready to make a change or do something different doesn't mean that everything is falling apart.

Let me give you an example. When I was at the point in my career where I wanted to leave and do something completely different, there were still things that were good about where I was. I sat down and made my "Good List" to clarify all the positive things about the job. Here is the list I came up with for my Good List.

- I had an excellent job with a good salary. It had been reasonably stable, and I had been able to move up and grow throughout the years.

- I had a fantastic team, the kind of team that worked together well. Each team member had valuable skillsets that balanced out our team, and they always delivered on the projects we had.
- I enjoyed the industry and the majority of the work I did. I was an expert with almost 20 years in real estate investment management and possessed an in-depth knowledge of the finance and technology aspects of my field.
- I had excellent benefits. I had one of the best pension and 401k packages that I had ever seen in my life and decent insurance coverage for my family.

It's your turn. I want you to think about all of the good things that are happening for you. What is going well in the area that you are trying to decide to change? Some of the things you put on your Good List might be things that you are going to miss or have to give up if you decide to make a change. Take a few minutes to make your Good List.

As you made your list, how did it feel? Were there things that you wrote down that you thought, how am I going to give that up? Am I going to find something better than what I have? Or did you start thinking, well maybe it isn't all that bad?

I shared with you several things that were good and going well for me when I was at the point in my career where I just wanted to get out. Someone from the outside might look in and say to me, "You've got this great job and, everything's going well for you. You've gotten a promotion, you have an amazing team, good benefits, and you like a lot of what you do. Why would you ever think about leaving?"

Well, that's when the bad comes in because not everything was so good. There's always some underlying things happening for everybody that are not so good. To get clear on all that was not so good, I had to sit down and create my "Bad List." Here is what I came up with:

- I worked 60-80 hours a week, and that became the expectation and norm.
- The company was going through reorganizations about every six months, which led to constant stress and cutbacks.
- My management changed three times in one year.
- There had been a culture change in the company since I had started, and it just wasn't the same environment it used to be.
- We had acquired a couple of other companies, and merging the groups and systems was not going smoothly.
- I wasn't able to go to many of my kid's school events because of work.
- My husband had threatened to throw my phone in the ocean many times when we were on vacation because I was tied to it 24/7 to respond to business questions.

Many things were going on that were bad, and I had to put them into perspective.

What is the bad going on for you right now? Why are you here reading this book and wanting to make a decision to change? What do you feel like is going on that's making you want to hit that reboot button.

Take a few minutes now to write down your Bad List.

____

____

____

____

____

____

____

____

____

____

____

____

Now that you know the good and the bad let's tear back that curtain and get to the ugly. The real truth of what's going on. Things that you probably aren't sharing with a lot of people other than a few that you trust. Many of you probably haven't even admitted the ugly truth to yourself.

Underneath it all, there's the ugly side of what's happening for you. The bad is kind of like when someone's throwing darts at you, each one hurts, but you can recover from it. The Ugly is when someone hits you with an arrow. It knocks you back on the ground, and it takes some time to recover. Sometimes you don't ever completely recover, it leaves a scar, and it's a wound you carry with you for a long time.

The Ugly Truth is something you have to understand and acknowledge before you can move forward. You can't just walk away from it and pretend like it never happened. It takes some time to heal from and may leave you limping for a while.

A few things that happened throughout my career led me to the path of knowing that I wanted to do something more and get out of the corporate world. I was burnt out with the politics of what was happening. So many decisions made just didn't make any sense. But there's one situation that was the nail in the coffin for me.

I was in middle management at the time, and we were going through yet another reorganization. Typically, I had a lot of input into what was going to happen in my area during a restructuring. My managers (I had a direct report manager and a separate functional area manager at the time) and I talked about what was going to happen in this particular case.

They came to me and told me that they wanted me to take on an expanded role with the upcoming reorganization. It wasn't anything official yet, but they wanted to get my thoughts on the group and how this would impact the rest of the team.

I was excited about the opportunity. I would be taking on another group of about 30 people and expanding my responsibilities. The discussions continued for weeks. There were many other departments involved, and they were trying to make all the changes at one time.

During this time, I found out I was pregnant. I had been through multiple miscarriages, so I wasn't going to tell anyone about my pregnancy until I hit the 12-week mark. The restructure kept getting dragged on and put off. I finally hit the 12th week of my pregnancy, and I knew I needed to tell my managers.

I went in and shared with my managers that I was pregnant, and of course, they were very excited and congratulated me. But then everything went silent. I was no longer invited to meetings or discussions about the reorganization. At first, I just thought they were going through some approvals, and it was only part of the waiting game. But it turned into weeks, and I started to wonder what was going on.

A few weeks later, I got a phone call from my direct manager. He asked me to come up to his office. Now, this was someone I had only been reporting to for six months, and we rarely met, so I knew that something was up.

I walked into his office, and sitting there was also my functional area manager. I had never actually met with both of them at the same time, so now I'm starting to wonder what is going on.

I sat down, and they told me that I was not getting the expanded role that they had told me about. I thought okay, maybe they decided not to make some of the changes and there'd be another opportunity. But then they proceeded to tell me that they were going to be taking away all my current direct reports. I was now going to be an individual contributor.

This doesn't make any sense, I thought as I sat there listening. Then the icing on the cake was that they were also moving me under another manager. It was someone who knew nothing about my industry, what I did, and who I did not particularly have the best relationship with. Plus, they were making some changes for the people who had worked directly for me that I didn't think were the right decisions for them. I was worried they wouldn't be successful in their new roles as it went directly against what they had told me they wanted.

I'm sitting there listening to this thinking that none of this makes sense. For years, I had worked so hard for this company, led some significant projects, and had high ratings. As I sat there, I started shaking. Once I knew they were done telling me all the changes, I just looked at them and said, "I need to walk away from this conversation right now before I say something I might regret."

I stood up, went back to my office, shut the door, and cried. I had never cried at work before. I barely ever cried outside of work. But I felt like I had been handed down a sentence for a crime I didn't commit. I had to find out why this was happening.

I pulled myself together and went back to talk to my managers again and asked them, "why was this decision made?" Their response hit me harder than before. They said, "Tami, we don't believe you deserve this. But it wasn't up to us."

It had already felt like I was starting to lose control of my career. But now I'm thinking if my managers don't even have control of my career, who is controlling it? Someone who barely knew me, just making these decisions without knowing what impact it has.

This situation was the arrow that knocked me down, and I had to figure out how to recover from it. This was my ugly truth. I had gone through what some might perceive as discrimination because I was pregnant or because someone who barely knew what I did, decided he didn't want me in that role.

I had lost control over my career, hit a glass ceiling, and realized that the company didn't value me the way I thought it did.

When you can recognize the ugly truth, then you can face it head-on. You can figure out if it's fixable or if you need to make a change.

What is your ugly truth? What is it that has hit you like an arrow that knocked you down? Write it down here.

After the situation at work, I felt like I needed to control my career and figure out what I wanted. What I realized is that what I wanted was not to be sitting there working for somebody else. It wasn't working 60 to 80 hours a week, helping someone else build their dream, but that I wanted to create my dream. That I wanted to be in control again and find the freedom I had been crazing. I had missed out on so much time with my family, and it was time to find a way to change that.

I had been so dedicated to my job and this company. The realization that regardless of what I put into it, they had the control to change my responsibilities at any given moment and didn't care how it impacted me or anyone else. This was a turning point for me; the arrow hit me, and I had to figure out how not just to heal but also to come out of it stronger and find a new path.

I didn't want people to know what had happened or how much it hurt me because I had been a strong female leader in the organization, and I didn't want anyone to see me as vulnerable. But inside, I was hurting. The bottled-up frustration started to have an impact on my health.

I hit a point where the stress, frustration, and the impact it was having on my health were the driving forces for me to make a change. It was time to decide to leave a job that had many great things going for it.

I'm sharing this story with you because I want you to know that you're not alone in this, that there are people that have gone through similar things, that have faced their ugly truth and have come out of it even stronger. Your situation may be different; you may encounter a different type of decision. Still, it doesn't matter what it is- you can apply this process to get to your ugly truth and evaluate that against the good and the bad to help you determine the right decision.

Once you decide, stay committed, and figure out the right steps to help you get there, which is what we will be covering in the rest of the book, so continue reading and learn how to turn this around for you.

Clarity to a Brighter Future

> *"Limitations live only in our minds. But if we use our imaginations, our possibilities are endless."*
>
> —Jamie Paolinetti

Growing up, we had three-wheelers that we would ride through the fields. I lived on a farm in Michigan, and when the fields were really dry, we used to do circles to make the dust fly up around us. The dust would be so thick that you couldn't tell which way to go to get back on the path. We'd have to stop for a few minutes until it cleared so that we could see again. If we turned the wrong way, we could end up in a ditch on one side or a pond on the other.

When your mind is spinning in circles, you create this cloud of dust surrounding you that blocks you from seeing what direction to go. You can't see what's even possible in the future or how to move past your current state to know where you should be going.

If you want to create a brighter future, you've got to stop spinning and let the dust settle so that you can see clearly. Or find a way to get above the dust so that you can look down and see the path.

One way to do this is a technique that I learned from Dean Graziosi, the author of ***Millionaire Success Habits*** and founder of several multi-million dollar companies, where you take yourself out of today and put yourself in the future. I want you to think about picking yourself up and moving one year into the future. Whatever day you are reading this, add one to the year and think about this exact day one year from now.

Visualize yourself standing there looking back over the past year. Imagine you've just had a fantastic year and ask yourself; What have I done in the last year? What does my life look like?

Imagine that you've just had the best year of your life. You've been able to transform many things that have been going on in your life this year. What have you accomplished? Where have you been? What has changed? What do you look like?

Maybe you got a new job, started a business, lost 20 pounds, fell in love, spent more time with your family, or took your dream vacation. Or perhaps you left a bad relationship, found more joy in your life, made more money, lost weight, or whatever would define what a year from now would look like if you decided to make a change and live your best life.

I want you to list everything that you think of when you visualized yourself one year from today having the best year of your life. Be specific about what you see and what you would want to happen in that year. You want to be clear about this and set the direction because when you are pointing yourself in the wrong direction, or you don't have a clear target, you're never going to get there. You need to see through all the dust currently in your way and visualize the track that lies ahead.

Take a few minutes to close your eyes and think about standing here a year from now and looking back at the amazing year you've just had. Where are you? What have you done in the last year? Where have you been? What have you let go of? What have you achieved? What does it feel like?

____

____

____

____

____

____

____

____

____

____

____

____

Can you see it? Can you feel what it was like?

If you have kids or ever been around a toddler, you know how obsessed they can be about something you don't want them to have. They go after the plant on the ground, try running for the stairs, or grab the toy that someone else is playing with, and regardless of how many times you tell them no, it doesn't stop them.

When you point out something to them and tell them to stay away from it, what happens? You've captured their attention, and now they want to crawl or walk right over to what you told them they couldn't have.

There's a time before they understand what "no" means or what consequences are that you have to redirect them to something else. You have to point them in the direction you want them to go or lead them to a different toy that's going to be okay for them to play with and keep their attention away from the other object that you don't want them to have. But the new thing has to be so much more fascinating and intriguing to appeal to them enough that they don't even think about that other object.

This exercise is your redirect toward the exciting new possibilities of what you could possess within the next year if you stayed focused on the right things, stopped dwelling on distractions, and avoid obstacles that pull you off course.

When a kid first starts riding their bike, if you point to a pothole in the road or that steep ditch to their side and tell them to watch out for that, what will they do? They are going to look to where you are pointing and go that direction, or they are going to get off balance and fall off the bike. Instead, if you show them the best path to ride on and exactly where they need to go to stay safe, they will focus on that path and not be looking into the ditch. Set focal points for them to reach, and it will keep their head up, and they will have fewer falls and learn the skill so much faster.

The same is true for you when you are trying to do something different, learn something new, or create a new habit. If you are always focused on where you are now, what is going wrong, and all the obstacles surrounding you, you will either head in the wrong direction or fall over and stop any progress. You have to stop pointing to things that aren't going right and start focusing on where you want to be.

If you didn't stop to do the exercise above, then stop reading now and go back and do it. You are reading this book because there is a decision you want to make. Or a change that you've been struggling with making. And this is one way for you to take yourself out of the current situation, put yourself in the future and look back to identify what your best year would look like if you stayed focused on the prize. How is that different than what you have today?

This exercise is a stepping stone to help you get to the best decision by knowing what you visualize for your better choice. It enables you to see that brighter future. If we can't see it first as a possibility, then it's not going to happen. If you're stuck, fixated on the present or the past, your future will bring you more of what you're currently focused on.

Most people will overestimate what they can do in a day or even a week, but they underestimate what they can do in a year. So I challenge you to think about that. What can you accomplish in this next year? What could happen for you?

It's time to decide to go for a brighter future, whatever that is for you. It's different for every single person. What is right for someone else doesn't make it right for you. You have to make the decision based on what is right for you.

Just because I left the corporate world to start my own business doesn't make it the right choice for everyone. There is a lot you need to consider before starting your own business. 45% of businesses fail within the first five years, so you have to want it if you're going to do it.

Just because your friends decide to get married, have kids, or leave their relationships, doesn't mean you follow their lead. It's is your life, and you have to do what is right for you in your current situation.

I want you to know that you have a brighter future, whatever that is for you. There is an abundance of things that could happen for you. If you decide to take ownership of where you are and decide to take action to make those things happen.

If I were to run into you a year from now, what will you be excited to tell that you have done in the last year?

____

____

____

____

____

____

____

____

____

____

____

____

Gathering Information for a Better Decision

"Questions are like alarm clocks, they wake you up."

—Gay Hendricks

We got our culture survey results back for our company, and it did not look so good. The company's results overall had gone down as a result of mergers and challenges that came along with mixing different cultures and leadership teams. But the technology team which I had just recently joined had one of the worst ratings in the organization.

The senior leaders got together to discuss how to address the issues and decided that we needed to put together a team to figure out how we could improve three of the lowest areas. I got a phone call shortly after that meeting, asking me to lead this culture change task force.

This was the second time that I had been sought out to lead a group to help initiate culture change within the organization. There was part of me that was honored to be selected, and another part that knew this was going to be a challenging project. Then they told me the three areas that I needed to focus on: learning, employee development, and leadership.

I wasn't shocked by these, but in the back of my mind I'm thinking, I have to come back to you, my bosses, and tell you what you are doing wrong as leaders??? This ought to be interesting.

Half of our senior leadership team in technology had come from a company that we acquired, and the other half were people who had been with the acquiring company for anywhere from fifteen to thirty-five years. The leaders had different styles, and it showed.

They gave me a team of twelve individuals to make up our task force. Most of them, like me, were in a management role and a couple of them were individual contributors. We sat down and talked about how we wanted to go about gathering information in order to determine what improvements we were going to propose.

We decided to hold small group meetings with all one hundred and seventy employees in the group. We wanted to hear from everyone and give people an opportunity to speak up.

We came up with a list of very specific questions we wanted to ask everyone. We made sure that no one had anyone in their meetings that reported to them so that people felt more comfortable speaking freely, and we held over forty meetings in just a few weeks.

The information we gathered during these meetings was critical for us to determine what actions leadership needed to take to make a difference, what things were going to move the needle in shifting the culturing and bringing these two once separate companies into one.

I remember sitting down with the senior leaders and the head of the department said, "I don't want to hear about people's requests to have bagels or pizza. Those things don't matter." I responded, "If you want to bring people together, there is no better way than having food. People bond over food." She gave me a glare, and I thought this is going to be interesting. It started out as a joke, but the feedback we got was people wanted to get rewarded for their work, have events that recognized major projects and find ways to get to know what the other teams were doing.

I was definitely not suggesting that food was going to fix all the culture problems, but people needed to be able to talk outside of the stressful meetings that were happening and actually get to know each other on a personal level. One of the things we implemented was a monthly lunch celebration. A team that was about to start or had just completed a big project got to share it with everyone else over a lunch and learn.

By asking the questions to all employees and opening it up to them to suggest solutions, we were able to get several doable steps that management could take to make an impact. We put together the top ten suggestions for each area, and I took them to the leadership team.

When you're faced with having to give your leadership team news about how their leadership isn't so great…it can be a little concerning. I went in armed with my list of solutions and the feedback we had received.

The biggest challenges within the organization stemmed from the management styles. We had a leader who no one really knew. We didn't have regular town halls, and so no one knew what her objectives were. There had been very little communication since the merger had happened over a year prior. Then there were a few leaders under her who were very direct and came across as rude and not caring for employees' wellbeing or opinions.

Surprisingly the conversation didn't go too bad. It would have been much worse had I not had all the data our task force had gathered and solutions prepared to make improvements. We were able to move forward with several solutions and started seeing feedback that small shifts were happening. There was still a long way to go, but we were able to take the first steps, see the results, and make shifts along the way.

When you're faced with a big shift that needs to happen, you have to gather information in order to really know the best way to move forward. There were many suggestions that people came up with that just our task force alone would have never thought of. It gave us more options and ideas.

The same applies when you are trying to make a better decision. You have to know your options and be able to choose the one that gets you better results. Begin by asking questions and gathering information. You may not always know what to ask, or sometimes you may not want to ask. You want to be given the answers without taking the time to ask the questions. Or you are afraid of what answers you will get.

The sooner you start asking the questions, the sooner you can wake up to better options and the truth. The sooner you see the truth, the sooner you can make a better decision.

It is important not to avoid what you do not want to hear. When you avoid the questions or options that you don't want to hear, you are closing yourself off to all your real options. When you do that, you will remain in a place of illusion and not be able to get out.

I hear people say all the time that they have no other option. I'm sure I've said this myself a few times, but I've learned that when you feel this way, it's because you just can't see any other options. It doesn't mean they aren't out there. So, if you find yourself saying you don't have any other options, just stop and smile and know that you simply aren't aware of all your options yet. This is a clear sign you need to start asking more questions.

When you are asking others questions and for their opinions on things, you need to be careful to not accept someone else's views as your reality. First, make sure you are asking people that you feel can guide you. Listen to what they say and then validate the information for yourself. Check the facts, determine if their views are swayed by their own circumstances that may be different from your reality.

When I wanted to move to a different state, I narrowed it down to two states that I was interested in. Then I made two lists. One was a list of things that I wanted in the place I moved to, and the other was a list of questions I had about each area. I started reaching out to people I knew in those areas and asking them questions to help me get clarity around where I should move.

When I was sought out for a job, I reached out to people who worked for the company to ask them what they liked and didn't like about it. I wanted to know about the culture, the leaders, and the benefits. I took the information I learned to help me make my decision.

Start by making a list of questions that you need to get answered to help you make a better decision and show you all your options.

____

____

____

____

____

____

____

____

You've got your list, but now who do you go ask? You want to make sure it is someone who knows the subject you have questions about. Someone who has been through what you are going through. Someone who will not just give you a nice and easy answer but will actually tell you the hard truth as well. When you get clear on your questions, the answers start showing up sometimes without you even asking.

A year after I left my corporate job, I won a ticket to go to one of Suzanne Evan's Business Accelerator Masterminds ("BAM") at a networking event I was at where she was the speaker. I had worked with some other business coaches prior to meeting her but hadn't seen as much success in my business as I had wanted to. I showed up to the BAM, not really sure what to expect, but I had my list of questions and intentions for what I wanted to get out of it.

When it was my turn for the hot seat, I shared what she calls the state of the union with the group. What my business is, what my offerings were, and what had been working.

Suzanne immediately launched into all the changes I needed to make and how to structure my business for more success. She said, "You've been doing all the right things but at the wrong time."

She had no hesitation in telling me exactly what I was doing wrong and how to fix it. It was a hard truth for me to hear as I had put so much time and effort into more advanced tactics that were not right for where I was in my business. I had followed the advice of people who were just trying to sell their programs and didn't necessarily care if it was the right strategy for me based on where I was in my business.

This is one of the reasons that I now focus so much on this with my clients starting a business so that they don't waste a lot of time and money on the wrong things. That's one of the reasons, so many businesses fail.

Who you ask is just as critical as what you ask. Remember that you have to put your own lens on what they are saying and not take everything everyone says as gospel. Do some research to figure out who the best people are to ask your questions to. Who has the expertise you are looking for? Who has gotten the results you want?

List out the people you can reach out to that have the knowledge and expertise that answer your questions. You may not know someone yet and need to write down the type of person you need to talk to. Then ask people you know if they know someone with that experience or search someone out. Or they may just pop into your life unexpectedly as Suzanne did for me.

____

____

____

____

____

____

Once you have your list of questions and who you are going to ask, set up a time to talk to them. Write down what they say. When you've finished all your inquiries, reflect back on your big takeaways, how it impacts your choice and the decision you come to.

____

____

____

____

____

____

Goals That Deliver

> *"If you want to be happy, set a goal that commands your thoughts, liberates your energy, and inspires your hopes."*
>
> —Andrew Carnegie

If I were to ask you if you want more money, I guarantee your answer would be "Yes."

If I gave you one dollar, would you be satisfied?

Probably not. But you said you wanted more money and you now have more money than before I gave you the dollar bill.

The problem is that you weren't specific enough. You didn't say I want one thousand dollars more or ten thousand dollars more or a hundred thousand dollars more. So how could you measure if you have more or not? You have got to be specific when it comes to setting your goals and deciding what you want.

"Some" and "more" are not numbers, and "soon" is not a time. When saying you want something, give it specific amounts and dates to measure by so that you know when you reach your goal.

Don't just say you want a new car. What kind of car? What color is it? What model is it? What year is it? We need specificity. You don't just say, "I want a new car," and have something pull up and think, "Okay, I'll deal with that."

When you aren't specific, when something shows up, like the one-dollar bill, you don't even recognize that it was showing up because you asked for more money. You think that you're not reaching your goals, and nothing is going the way you want. You start to complain about it, and when you complain about it, you become victims of it. And the minute you become a victim of it, you've lost your confidence in your ability to get what you want.

When I started my business and was still working full time, I decided that there was a precise number I wanted to hit for my bonus that year if I was going to turn in my resignation and go full time into my business. I wrote down the number and thought about it often. It was significantly higher than any bonus I had ever gotten in the past, so it wasn't a given that I would get it.

And guess what?

The bonus I got was exactly that number. Not $1 more or $1 less. The exact amount that I had on my list of goals! If I wanted a sign, it was time to quit and go into my business full time; this was it.

I can give you many examples just like this, where I have set a very specific goal and was able to manifest exactly what I wanted. The power of what we think, write, and say is magnificent. The keys are to be clear on what you need, be specific in the results, and the outcome you want to get, and by when.

You want a better job. Okay. Does that mean your salary is $1,000 more or $100,000 more? Does that mean that you work ten hours less or different hours? Does it mean it's closer to your house? Does it mean you have a boss who respects you and your value? Does it mean you are doing different work? What does a better job mean to you?

You want a better relationship with your spouse. What does that mean? Does it mean you're not going to fight ten times a day, you're going to reduce that to nine times a day? That would be better, right? Nine fights are better than ten. So what does a better relationship mean to you? What does that look like?

You want to become an entrepreneur. What does that look like for you? What steps are involved, and when are you going to get them done? What is your income goal and by when?

What does that brighter future look like for you? People who set specific and measurable goals outperform those that set vague goals.

List out the top goals that will help you get to that brighter future a year from now and bring about the change you desire. Be specific about what you want and by when you want to achieve it.

____

____

____

____

____

____

____

____

CHAPTER 7

Confidence

"Our deepest fear is not that we are inadequate. Our deepest fear is that we are powerful beyond measure."

—Marianne Williamson

Nothing is more attractive than someone who's confident. We attract to ourselves based on how confident we are. People believe you or not based on how confident you are. They hire you based on your confidence. When you don't have confidence, you don't act. A confident person steps out and is willing to risk.

A lack of confidence makes you less attractive to do business with. It makes you doubt yourself, and others doubt you as well. It keeps you from getting the results you want.

Confidence is something that holds people back in so many ways. When you think about where you are right now, are you confident in who you are? Are you confident in what you do? Are you confident with the decision you are making? Are you confident with what your next step is?

Webster's definition of confidence is "a feeling or consciousness of one's powers or of reliance on one 's circumstances; faith or belief that one will act in a right, proper or effective way."

Confidence grows with clarity and accomplishments. Until you get complete clarity on what it is you want to do, your confidence will falter. You will continuously run into the fears and stumbling blocks that will hold you back because you don't have the complete faith and belief that this is what you're meant to do.

The Greatest Version of You

> *"It's not who you are that holds you back, it's who you think you are not."*
>
> —Denis Waitley

To develop your confidence, first, you've got to break your old habits and beliefs. Harvard did a study that revealed that 45% of what we do every day is based on habit and done unconsciously. You don't even think about so much of what you do, and you continue in the same cycle all the time. Sometimes those habits are good habits and other times they are not so good habits. We first have to become aware and conscious of those habits before we can change them.

One of the negative habits that most people have is negative self-talk. The negative self-talk can hold you back in so many ways and has a lasting impact that takes some shifts to move through. It may be something inside you that you keep telling yourself, something you hear from others that are not supportive of what you do, or the constant complaining you are doing when things aren't going your way.

That negative self-talk may have started initially because of what someone else said to you. It may not have even been true, but you heard it, and now you believe it.

When I was young, people used to say to me all the time that I was shy. I started to believe it and took it on as my identity. When people came up and started talking to me, I would smile and say only a few words to reply to their questions. They would turn to my parents and say, oh, she's so shy, but she has a beautiful smile. I heard this over and over again, and it started to impact how I would respond. People didn't expect me to speak up anymore, so why should I?

The truth was that I wasn't shy; I just like to sit back, observe, and listen before I speak up. I want to hear what is going on with others. I'm an excellent listener. I like to understand what others are going through and speak when I feel I can add to the conversation. Small talk doesn't come naturally to me. When I ask someone how they are doing, I want to know deep down how they are, not the surface answer of good. Meaningful conversations drive me to talk more, but the small talk will keep me quiet unless I force myself to participate.

I'm sure you've gone through similar situations where someone perceives something about you, but it isn't exactly the truth. They may think you are rude, but the truth is you're just direct and straight forward. Someone may have told you that you don't have what it takes to do something, but they haven't seen the real drive you have within.

It can take time to uncover the real truth underneath these lies and stop the negative self-talk and the complaining. But you first have to recognize what you are telling yourself or someone else is telling you that is holding you back.

I had a client who was sharing her story with me and telling me some of the ideas she had for her future business. During our conversation, she repeatedly said, "I'm not the expert." After hearing her say how she didn't think she could start a business, write a book, do trainings and many other specific things related to the work she had been doing, I finally asked her how long she had been doing the type of work she did.

She replied, "I've been doing this for sixteen years."

I replied, "Do you know how long it takes to become an expert?"

She shook her head, no.

I said, "It takes around ten thousand hours to become an expert, which is about five years if you work full time or ten years if you're working part-time. You are technically an expert in this area."

She had been telling herself this story over and over again. It came out in the form of I don't have the degree, I don't have the certifications, and I don't have the book to validate my experience. She had sixteen years of real-life experience, but because she didn't have the certification on our wall, she told herself she wasn't good enough.

Let me ask you. Who would you rather learn from, the person who has spent sixteen years working in a specific area and has real-life experience testing their theories and applying what they know, or a person who wrote a book, has a degree but hasn't implemented any of it?

I know that I want to hear from the person who has applied it. Now I'm not trying to say that getting a degree or certification doesn't help you, and in the right fields, it does. But in her case, this was just a story she was telling herself that was holding her back.

Here are some of the negative self-talk that she was telling herself:

- I'm not an expert.
- I don't have what it takes.
- No one will listen to me.
- I'm not good enough.
- I don't deserve to have more than I have now.
- No one believes in me.

Have you told yourself these kinds of stories in the past; That you're not the expert, that you don't have the experience, that you're not meant for this?

She is not alone in this. We've all been there. We've all told ourselves countless stories about why we can't make a change, do something else, or why we don't deserve something better than what we have. The negative self-talk is what's hurting us. You've got to stop with the negative self-talk. You've got to shift your focus because where your attention goes, energy flows. So if you are focusing on the negative, the bad, and the ugly right now, that is where the energy is going to flow, and you're going to create more negative in your life.

Think about the change you want to make and what is holding you back. Are there things that you are telling yourself that are getting in the way? Do you have a story that someone else told you that is now stealing your confidence?

When you can identify these negative self-talk patterns and reframe them, you can make massive shifts in your confidence. I want to help you get rid of these so that you can make a lasting change.

In this exercise, you will list out the negative things you've been telling yourself that are holding you back. The stories that keep you from feeling confident. The feelings that come up that keep you from moving forward. Take ten minutes to think about the change you want to make and all the excuses you've been making. Write them down below. Then throughout this next week, as you find yourself saying or thinking, other negative thoughts come back and add them to this list.

____

____

____

____

____

____

____

____

____

____

Would you ever say to your children, "You're not good enough. You don't deserve this." No one believes in you. No! Never! I know I couldn't. The thought of saying something like that to my kids makes me feel sick and sad.

So why do we do this to ourselves?

We've developed these habits that are trying to keep us where we are. There may have been times where those voices kept us safe and protected. But those same voices are holding us back and taking away the power that we have deep down.

Now that you know what's holding you back, you can start to replace them. To turn these around, you need to come up with the truth that contradicts these negative things you are saying to yourself.

For my client who was telling herself that she didn't have what it takes to start a business in an area that she had sixteen years of experience in; she had to turn these around to say:

- I am the expert.
- My experience gives me more than enough knowledge to teach others.
- I am good enough.
- I have what it takes to be successful.
- I deserve to be successful.

How can you turn your negative self-talk around? What are the new positive affirmations that you can start saying to yourself to eliminate the negative self-talk? Here are some more examples of affirmations that are commonly needed.

- I am powerful.
- I am wise.

- I am ambitious.
- I am deserving of _______________ (this promotion, a great relationship, better health).
- I have what it takes to _______________ (start my own business, lose the weight, get in shape, change jobs, build a better relationship).
- I know how to make the most out of opportunities.
- I am beautiful.
- I am confident.
- I am courageous.
- I am consistent.
- I am committed.
- I am unstoppable.

Another way to do this is to look at each of the negative affirmations you wrote above and replace each one with the opposite more empowering belief.

What new affirmations do you need to hear to empower you to make the decision and change that you desire? You can take any or all of these examples, and create more of your own.

Write out your new positive affirmations below.

____

____

____

____

____

____

____

____

____

Now that you have your list of the negative beliefs and your new empowering affirmations I want you to commit to changing these by doing an exercise for the next thirty days. For the first seven days take the list you wrote for your negative self-talk and look in the mirror and say each of those to yourself. After you say each one stop and replace it with the new more empowering belief.

After seven days of doing the replacement, then you can drop the negative self-talk and just start saying your positive affirmations for the remaining thirty days. Look yourself in the eye when you say them and feel what a difference it makes. As you say them feel it in your body and make the gestures you would feel if you truly believed these things. Get excited and say them with power and conviction.

This exercise is so powerful, and you will only understand the impact it has by doing it yourself and committing to doing this for the next thirty days. Any time you hear yourself saying something negative either out loud or to yourself, stop and correct yourself with your new positive affirmation that replaces the negative self-talk you are used to saying.

The first time I did a similar exercise where we had to say our affirmations to ourselves in the mirror, I was doing a program with Lisa Nichols, the founder and CEO of Motivating the Masses, Inc. She calls it "Mirror Work" when you have to face yourself with your truth. This exercise brought tears to my eyes. It's hard to believe some of the negative things that we tell ourselves, but when you look yourself in the eye and say it, it has a huge impact.

I realized that I couldn't look in my own eyes and lie to myself. It's pretty much impossible. I do this with my kids all the time. When I think they're telling me something that's isn't true, they're trying to trick me, or they're just not listening, I say "look me in the eyes." And they know they can't get away with it. Mama knows them, and they know they can't lie to me. They might try to avert their eyes, or they come up with a different story.

Looking in your own eyes changes everything about the story you tell yourself. When you're looking into your eyes, you're looking into your soul, and you see who you are.

Try looking in your eyes in the mirror and saying the things you wrote down for your negative self-talk. Then replace it by telling yourself the positive and true statements. This activity will help you shift parts of you that are blocking your confidence so that you can accept the greatest version of yourself.

Your Physical State Determines Your Confidence

> *"I have a confidence about my life that comes from standing tall on my own two feet."*
>
> —Jane Fonda

If you want to improve your confidence, you also need to change your physical state. How you sit, stand, move, and feel has an impact on how you show up. Emotion is created by motion. The moves that you make, how you present yourself, and the state that you are in, create your emotion.

If you are walking into an interview and your head is hanging, your shoulders are slumped, and you give a light handshake, the person interviewing you is going to think that you have no confidence whatsoever. When you stand up straight, take a few minutes before you go in to do the superman pose and give a friendly firm handshake you will create the sense that you are more confident in who you are and you're your abilities to do the job.

Think about your physical state throughout the day. Where are you showing up with confidence, and your body reflects that and where are you feeling tired, slumped over in your chair and not reflecting as someone who is confident.

When you walk into your office in the morning, are you dragging yourself to go in with your coffee in your hand, hoping it gives you enough energy to make it through the day? Or are you excited about what the day is going to bring? When you get up on a stage, do a Facebook live, present at work, or are talking to a prospect, are you smiling, standing tall with your shoulders back, and showing your enthusiasm about your subject matter? When you get home to your family at night are you so worn out that you just plop down on the couch and barely say a word to anyone or are you hugging your spouse and kids, smiling and grateful that you have them to come home to them.

How you show up makes a huge difference in how you feel and how others perceive you. If you want people to believe you are confident, then you have to show up like you are. The fastest way to change your emotions is to change your body.

When you have a stressful day, have a conversation that leaves you frustrated, or are around someone that drains your energy, you have to be able to let that go before you move on with your day. Letting go of that negative energy will allow you to move on with your day without carrying all of that with you.

One of the ways to do that is what I call the brush off. It is an energy clearing technique where you take your hands and brush off your entire body. You use the palms of your hand to brush off your body. This action helps to remove any energy that might be on you from previous situations. Starting with your arms, then your torso, and moving down to your legs. It's like when you get lint on your black pants from the white napkin at a restaurant, and you brush it away.

The brush away also helps to clear the energy so that you can go into a new situation with a calm and open perspective. I use this technique between clients so that I do not take the energy of one into a session with another. I also use it before I get up on stage to help me be fully in the energy of the audience, and anytime I feel a bit drained from a situation.

Try it now and see how it feels.

You may feel a slight tingling throughout your body or a sense of renewal as you brush off lingering energy. This brushing away is something you can do in just a minute to make a big difference in your day. You can slip into the bathroom after a bad meeting and brush it away, or before you walk in the door at night to leave any work energy behind you as you greet your family.

You can also just get up and move when you find yourself feeling stuck, frustrated, or like you've lost your momentum. Just getting up and going for a walk, stretching, or having a little dance party can change your state, increase your confidence in the moment and leave you feeling refreshed.

At our house, you will find frequent dance parties in our living room. After going to Tony Robbin's Business Mastery, my husband started playing dance music in our office in the mornings to get into state before he would start seeing patients. Since we work out of the same office, I would get up and dance with him if I was free. There have been several times when I'm in the middle of a coaching session, and all of a sudden, the music starts pounding from the next room, and my client wonders, what is that?

If you've been to a Tony event, you know what I'm talking about. If you haven't, Tony plays extremely loud music with lights going, and everyone is standing on their chairs, dancing and going crazy. The right music and movement change your state quickly.

Throughout your day today, make a conscious effort to look at your body language and what it is reflecting. What do you notice? How can you make improvements? What situations are draining you and making an impact on your physical state? When do you need to do the brush off to clear some energy, go for a walk, or play some music?

____

____

____

____

____

____

____

____

____

____

____

Surrounded by Certainty

"The certainty within our spirit made the dream reality."
—Lailah Gifty Akita

I woke up one morning in a sweat - shaking. Feeling like the dream that I just had was still happening. I laid there for a few minutes, trying to catch my breath and replaying in my mind everything I could remember about this dream.

I got up and walked into my daughter's room to make sure she was there. She was still asleep, and I kissed her on the cheek. Then I went to my other daughter's room and laid down beside her as she slept. While quietly admiring the beauty of a sleeping child, overwhelming gratitude for their health came over me.

Throughout the day, I couldn't stop thinking about the nightmare I had. I started to wonder what it meant. Even though I knew it wasn't real, it had scared me, and I couldn't get it out of my mind.

I didn't know how to move past it. I didn't know what it meant. It was one of those dreams that left me shaken to the core. What's more, this was the second dream I had in the past month that left me feeling this way.

I knew that they were trying to tell me something. I was sure there was something more to the dreams. I decided it was imperative to find the answers and understand what these dreams meant.

I was in this group of coaches and healers, and I figured somebody in that group must know someone who could help. So I posted in the group and asked who had experience interpret dreams.

A few people responded with recommendations, but one of the ladies I had met just a few months prior reached out and said, "You need to talk to my husband, The Monk. He can help you find the answers to your dreams."

I knew she was a sweet and caring woman, but I didn't know much about her husband. I agreed to meet with him, and she set up a time for us to talk over zoom as they lived halfway across the world in New Zealand. I didn't find out until later that he had been a coach for some incredibly famous people and had just taken a year off of working with anyone.

I got on a call with him, and he started asking me about the dreams. He asked me more questions about my current situation and what I wanted out of life.

I shared with him that I felt constrained by my job. I wanted more flexibility to be there for my kids. I had a desire to travel but wanted to do it on my terms and not only when and where the company wanted to send me. I wanted the freedom to be my own boss and to take control of my career.

He asked me to peer directly into the camera with my eyes very close, as he wanted to look beyond my eyes. He did some other tests as well, and our conversation brought me to tears. I could see how these dreams were just signs that it was time for a change, but he showed me how I was still clinging to the things of the past.

There was a single question during this conversation that changed everything for me.

He said to me, "What is more important to you, security or freedom? Because everything you're saying to me tells me you want freedom. But you're clinging to the security that you have."

At that moment, I realized that what I wanted more at that time was security. I liked knowing I had a steady paycheck. It was fulfilling a need by giving me a level of certainty and helped me feel safe and secure.

I had to figure out how to make the shift from security to freedom. How I could take the risk necessary to find the freedom I had been longing for while also filling my need to provide financial protection for my family.

There was still a lack of certainty and confidence that I could make the transition and not resort to selling our house or giving up the lifestyle that we had. The examples of entrepreneurship I learned as a child were hard work and uncertainty, and they were still impacting my outlook on what was possible.

Growing up on a farm gave me a one-sided perspective of working for yourself. I saw my dad working sixteen-hour days and doing hard manual labor, which paid off with bountiful crops for many years. But there were also years when we'd have a drought or a flood, and it would wipe out most of the crops.

It was devastating at times to see how all that work could be for nothing. To bear witness to my family's struggle to figure out how they were going to survive until next year's crops came. We always got by, and my mom would do odd jobs and eventually went back to school to become a nurse in order to provide more stability for our family. Growing up, this had been my experience of entrepreneurship, which ended in my dad selling the farm and going into real estate.

I knew that I needed to change my level of confidence to be successful. There were two things I had to do to increase my level of certainty.

First, I had to take a look at the security I was clinging to and develop a plan for how I would still meet that human need for certainty in my life and feel safe in my decisions. For me, that meant having enough savings to last me a year to get my business started.

Secondly, I had to surround myself with successful entrepreneurs who had done what I wanted to do. I needed to see what was possible and understand what it took to become confident that I was making the right choice.

You might face a different decision, but something is holding you back from making a choice you want to make. We talked about what you are getting out of the situation in chapter 2 and how you might replace that need or desire.

Now I want you to think about who you can surround yourself with that has already been through the change you wish to make.

We become most like the people we surround ourselves with. You have to start looking at who is in your chain of influence. Those people that are helping you to build your stories or are killing your dreams.

If you want to get better results, then you need to find others that have already achieved those results and learn from them. See what they have done right and learn from the mistakes that they have already made so that you don't end up making the same mistakes.

Surround yourself with people who are supportive and care about you accomplishing the things that you desire.

For me that meant finding the right coaches that had made the transition from employee to entrepreneur and learning from them. I also started working with accountability partners who were trying to accomplish the same things as me so that I had people to mastermind with and work through challenges with that were going through similar things.

You need to have a supportive community around you and experts in whatever you are going through to guide you through it. You need to surround yourself with certainty and that means having the right support in place.

Make a list of the people you know that you can reach out to for guidance, coaching, or mentoring that can show you how to do it successfully. Who has gotten positive results after making the change? Who else do you know going through a similar change that you could setup accountability with?

You may not know the expert yet and have to do some research to find the right person. That's okay. Just write down the specific type of person you need to find. Then you can start asking around and doing your research to find the right expert.

____

____

____

____

____

____

Acknowledge Your Accomplishments

"We ask ourselves, 'Who am I to be brilliant, gorgeous, talented, fabulous?' Actually, who are you not to be?"
—Marianne Williamson

I had a woman come to me who had started her business but wasn't getting many clients. As we were talking, she was timid and unsure of herself. When she spoke about what she did, you could hear some excitement in her voice, but then it would be followed with what if I take on too much, what if I try and don't succeed, or my husband wants me to get a job because he doesn't think I will ever make any money at this.

She was beating herself up inside, and it showed. She had incredible talent, but she didn't believe in herself. Her desire to help others was strong but not as strong as all the fears that came up for her.

What she didn't realize was that her husband was only reflecting back to her the insecurity she was feeling. Men are protectors, and if they sense that you are not confident and feel secure with your decisions, they will tell you to do something else or try to get you out of the situation, so you don't get hurt. However, if you approach them with a clear objective and stand by it 100%, they are more likely to support you. Once she was able to identify what was holding her back and gain more confidence in herself, his belief in her grew as well.

To get there, she first had to recognize the greatness within her and turn all the negative self-talk around. I started reflecting back to her what she was saying and reframing some of her comments. Digging deeper into where those thoughts were originating.

She was a coach and healer and had been dabbling at it for years, but life was always getting in the way, and she never got any real momentum. She had gotten amazing results with the clients that she had worked with, but yet her confidence level was so low that she wasn't attracting clients. I suggested she start reading her client testimonials every day to remind herself of how great her work is.

This daily exercise helped to rebuild her confidence in her business and the passion she had for it. It didn't take long for her to see a massive shift in her confidence and start seeing better results in her business.

One of the exercises I have found to be so impactful in acknowledging the greatness within you is to write down 50 accomplishments you have had. These can be things you are proud of that you have done, challenges you have overcome, or achievements you have received. Don't stop until you get at least 50. You'll find the first 10-20 come relatively easy, and then you start to slow down and have to think about what you've done and things for which you are proud.

When your list is complete, read it aloud to someone else. Stand up tall and be proud as you read it. Notice what feelings come up for you as you read each one. If you want to take this a step further, you can take these and create a brag book that you keep to remind yourself of your greatness when you need to build up your confidence.

Each time you consciously let yourself enjoy your accomplishments, see your creativity, appreciate the money you have, or feel the love in your life, the more you open up your capacity for more of it. So go celebrate these accomplishments!

Start writing down your list of accomplishments now, and don't stop until you get to 50.

1. ______________________________
2. ______________________________

3. ______
4. ______
5. ______
6. ______
7. ______
8. ______
9. ______
10. ______
11. ______
12. ______
13. ______
14. ______
15. ______
16. ______
17. ______
18. ______
19. ______
20. ______
21. ______
22. ______
23. ______
24. ______
25. ______
26. ______
27. ______
28. ______
29. ______
30. ______
31. ______
32. ______

33. ____
34. ____
35. ____
36. ____
37. ____
38. ____
39. ____
40. ____
41. ____
42. ____
43. ____
44. ____
45. ____
46. ____
47. ____
48. ____
49. ____
50. ____

CHAPTER 8
Courage

"What could we accomplish if we knew we could not fail?"
—Eleanor Roosevelt

Someone came up to me and said, "Aren't you scared?" Then someone else came up and said to me and said, "Wow, that takes a lot of courage. Aren't you scared?" And someone else said, "That takes a lot of guts. Are you scared?" When I gave my notice and told people that I was leaving my job to start a business, the biggest question I got was, "Aren't you scared?"

The decision I made seemed scary to many people. Leaving a twenty-year career to start a business was just unimaginable for some and downright frightening to others.

My response to them was, "I wouldn't be doing it if I was stuck in fear." But I didn't get to the place of having the courage to leave overnight. It was a process. I went through the steps that I am sharing with you in this book.

When I turned in my resignation, I had just gotten a promotion to head the real estate technology for what was the third-largest real estate investment management company in the world. If I were to look back at my career and what I had been working for, this was it. I was in the role that I had spent years working towards, but it wasn't what I wanted anymore. It came with a cost that was too much for me at that time in my life.

It took a lot of courage and confidence for me to leave. But I had 100% faith and belief that my coaching business was exactly what I was meant to do and that it was going to be successful. That confidence didn't happen overnight. I had been working on building my business for over a year while still working full time and getting my coaching certification. It had been a crazy busy year, but it also helped me realize that if I wanted something badly enough, I would do whatever it took to get it.

First, and probably the step that took me the longest, was clarity. Figuring out what I wanted to do and what business I was going to start. Once I knew that I was meant to be a success coach to help others through similar challenges and overcome those tough decisions, it was just a matter of putting the right steps in place to make it happen.

Of course, I had fears come up along the way. Wondering if I had enough experience if I was good enough at it, and having to overcome the fear of marketing and putting myself out there. But these were things that I worked on one step at a time. I had to find the courage to take the first step and then the next step and then the next until it got to me to the place where I knew it was time to leave the comfort of my job and venture out on my own.

When you take the right steps, the fear turns into excitement, and you can't resist but to move forward. Fear starts to dissipate when you are fully engaged in what you are doing and the impact it has.

Gay Hendricks in ***The Big Leap*** describes fear as excitement without the breath. When you hold your breath, excitement turns into fear. If you take big easy breaths when you feel fear, you can breathe through it and turn it into excitement. Fear and excitement create the same sensations in your body and get your adrenaline moving.

If you need a little nudge to finally take that first step, then this is me nudging you. Find that courage within you to take action and move forward.

Does it mean the first step will always be the right step? No, it does not. But even a failure is a motion that keeps you trying again, only you try again differently.

Overcome Your Story

> *"If you believe it will work out, you'll see opportunities. If you believe it won't, you will see obstacles."*
>
> —Wayne Dyer

I shared with you earlier how I hit that point in my career while I was pregnant that shook me to the core in many ways. There was a point when I realized that in some ways, it was happening for me and not to me. Even though I may have felt that they made the decision based on the wrong things, I had to turn this around and try to find some positive in it.

When it happened, I told myself stories that I wasn't good enough, that I wasn't part of the boy's club, and that I had hit a glass ceiling. I had to have the courage to let go of the story and look at what the situation could bring for me. Where could I go from there? How could I find some positive to come out of it?

I don't think I'd be writing this book if I hadn't gone through that situation because it woke me up to realize that I wanted more out of my career. It set me on a journey to figure out my bigger why and brought me to starting my coaching business. Sometimes it takes a significant incident like that for us to get pushed farther than we wanted to in order to see that it's time to take a step in a different direction.

Sometimes the universe gives us a little nudge, and other times, it hits us over the head. Let's face it, there are times in our lives where all we need is that little push. And we're like okay I hear you; I see you; I'm going to do it. Other times a little nudge just isn't enough, and you get hit over the head and knocked down. It wakes you up and makes you look at things with a new perspective. You start to realize you need to make a change; you need to get out and do something different.

To move forward after a difficult situation, you first have to overcome your story. You have to realize that it may be happening for you and not to you. You need to find the good that can come from the bad.

If you've been a victim and you continue to say that you are a victim, then that is what you will be. Your story dictates your reality, not just in the past but for your future. As soon as you can change your story, you can change your life.

If your story is that you tried something and it didn't work, so now you think nothing ever works, then nothing will ever work. If you turn this story around, learn from what didn't work, and adjust your approach, then you will have more success the next time.

It takes a lot of courage to let go of the story your holding onto and figure out how you can turn it around. It's time to release it. It's time to divorce the old story. You don't want to be one of those people who gets a divorce and keeps going back to their ex and never ultimately moves on. This is about divorcing your story and not turning back. Let go of the old story so that you can heal those wounds.

What is the story you've been telling yourself? How can you find something useful in that story or turn it around to make the outcome better? Think about the ugly truth you wrote down in Chapter 6. How is this possibly happening for you and not to you? Take a few minutes to reflect on a difficult situation you've faced and how you need to overcome the story and find a new perspective.

____

____

____

____

____

____

To completely let go of your story, sharing it is essential. Having the courage to tell someone your story, how it set you back, how you have found a way to turn it around, and how you are moving forward from it. Find at least one person that you can share this with today. Who is that going to be?

____

What Are You Waiting For?

"Before you can soar, you must first take off."

—Unknown

Many of you are in a waiting story. You're saying I'm just going to wait.

No!

It's time to start living your life each day. Stop waiting!

It's just silly for you to be telling yourself, well, I'll wait until I feel better. I'll wait until the kids leave. I'll wait until I get a new house. I'll wait until I start a new job. I'll wait until someone else says yes or finally permits me. I'll wait until I get a certificate or a degree. I'll wait until I'm ___ years old.

Do not wait!

Tomorrow is a new chapter. You don't have to wait for months or years or even decades. Start now. It's a choice you've got to make.

By telling yourself you are waiting on something, it's just a way for you to avoid the decision and let your fear keep you where you are.

The longer you wait, the more restless you become inside. The more things you put off and say you are waiting on, the more it stacks up and creates discomfort. Your mind starts to think, well, I know I want these things, and I know they're important to me, but I'm not taking action towards getting them. And this starts to build an internal distrust with yourself. You begin to believe that you will not work towards any of the things you want.

Many people stay in discouragement instead of working towards a better future because they're living in the self-distrust. It's not because they are bad but because their minds and bodies tell them in the background to do these things. Their mind is thinking, I know these are good things and the right things to do, but then they have a bad day or are feeling bad about themselves. So instead, they decide to go binge watch Netflix.

They are not doing what they know they should be doing. They're not the person they know they could be. They are not moving forward to their full potential.

Each thing you wait on is like stacking up weights on you, and eventually, when you stack up enough weights, you start to crumble under pressure.

Waiting is a way of hurting yourselves. The longer you wait, the more hurtful it is to your character and your identity. You have to be able to trust yourself to do what you know is right for your life.

I want you to ask yourself, what have you been waiting for?

Have you been waiting to have a difficult conversation with your spouse or your kid or your employee? Have you been waiting to start a business, a book, or a new endeavor? Have you been waiting to start working out or eating better?

You've been telling yourself that you were going to wait until everything is perfect, and all the stars align. But your brain is telling you that you are full of it. You know that you're waiting because you're scared, and you don't trust yourself. Stop waiting for things to be perfect because they will never be perfect.

I know people who have been married for twenty or thirty years, and they tell me that they haven't had a real relationship in over ten years. They say they are waiting for the kids to leave. For some of them, they have no intention of ever changing the relationship. They are comfortable the way it is, living with someone more of a roommate than a spouse.

I'm not judging them, and I'm not trying to encourage divorce, but something has to change if they want any prospect of a fulfilling relationship. It's time to stop waiting and decide to do something.

Decide to do everything you can to make your marriage work for the next ninety-days and commit one hundred percent to it. Don't let yourself give up during that time and try things you have never tried before. Be entirely dedicated to making it work and see what happens. You will know after that ninety days if there is any hope of it changing. But you've got to decide to stop putting off dealing with it and either go all in or let them go.

When I left my corporate job, I had several people ask me why I didn't wait until they let me go? It was a reflection back on them as to what they were doing. They were waiting for the company to go through another reorganization and figured their number would be up soon for the layoffs. Some of them waited years for this to happen; others are still there working and waiting for their package. The irony is that those that did get let go were then ticked off that it happened to them even though they thought it was better to wait. They didn't have a plan for what to do next because they were too busy waiting.

I'd rather be in control of my destiny. I'd rather be able to choose when I leave and not have someone else tell me that I'm fired. There are just some things that are not worth the wait.

To overcome the waiting game, I want you to write out a "Stop Waiting" list. This is the list of things that you are going to Stop Waiting to do. Here are some examples:

- I will stop waiting to start writing that book that I was going to write when I retired.
- I will stop waiting to tell my spouse that I love them even though we may be in the middle of a fight.
- I am going to stop waiting to look for another job.
- I am going to stop waiting to start my business.
- I am going to stop waiting to spend more time with my kids and improve our relationship.
- I am going to stop waiting to eat healthier and lose weight.
- I am going to stop waiting to call my friend or family member.

It can be big or small things. Things you've been dreaming about or something you just know you need to do. Just because you're busy doesn't mean everything has to wait. You need to be able to trust yourself to take action towards the things that are going to matter most.

It's your turn. Make your Stop Waiting list.

____

____

____

____

Whose Decision Is It

"No one can make you feel inferior without your consent."
—Eleanor Roosevelt

Several years ago, a friend told me about an employee issue they had in their practice. The employee had started off being happy and participating, and then she started to get mopey and frustrated easily. Her quality of work kept deteriorating. She started spending a lot of time on social media and doing things that weren't productive for the doctor's office, or her. And since she was in a managerial position in their business, it was starting to affect other employees and processes as well.

Their initial response was that they didn't want to fire her. They liked her as a person and didn't want things to get ugly.

Here's the thing, she was miserable at the job too but didn't want to leave them stuck without a manager. This dragged out six months to a year, which was way longer than it should have. All because neither one of them would take the action that would have made them all happier.

The employee ended up getting Lyme disease and proceeded to steal forty thousand dollars from them. She used the doctor's medical license to order special medicine without asking. It ended up being a complete nightmare for them.

They thought they'd just wait for her to leave, and instead, she started taking advantage of her position and stealing from them. If they had decided to address her behavior earlier when they first started seeing signs, none of this would have happened.

The point is that it is your decision to make.

This doesn't just apply to your employees. This applies to every area of your life. If it impacts you, then it's your decision to make. You can sit around waiting for someone else to do something, avoid the decision because you're afraid of hurting someone, or say that you can't do something because someone else won't let you. But if those are your excuse, then you have to at least own your part in it and be okay with it.

Be okay with having an employee who steals from you because you're too afraid to address the issue or fire them. Be okay with being in a bad relationship because you don't think you have the right to leave even though they've cheated, lied, or abused you. Be okay with the boss you don't trust because you don't have the courage to make a change. Be okay with waiting years for someone else to make up their mind.

If you're not okay with those things, realize you have a decision to make, and no one else will make it for you.

Where have you been saying that it isn't your decision to make or not deciding for fear of hurting someone?

____

____

____

How can you own that situation and make a better decision?

____

____

____

Take the First Steps

"By the yard it's hard. By the inch, it's a cinch."

—Unknown

It's time to stop wishing and start taking action. You can only get past the fears by taking action. Without clarity on what is possible, it is hard to take that step to overcome those fears.

Go back and look at the goals that you laid out that you want to achieve in Chapter 6 and your Stop Waiting List from earlier in this chapter and write down three action steps that you're going to take over the next thirty days that will help you reach those goals.

The first action item you are going to write down is one that you will do within the next twenty-four hours. Don't delay this any longer! Do one thing today that will be a step in the right direction. For you, that might be getting up and going for a twenty-minute walk, saying no to the dessert today, or picking up the phone and calling somebody that can support you. You may find someone to help hold you accountable or set up a time to have a difficult discussion you've been putting off. Something doable today that will be a small first step to your bigger goal.

Do you have the courage to say YES to one action step today? Do you have the courage to commit to what you want? Do one thing today that shows you are ready to say yes and commit to finding the courage to make it happen.

The second action item you are going to list is something you can complete in the next week. Taking a look at the goal that you have set, what can you do within the next seven days to move you closer to that goal.

The third action item will be something you can do within 30 days. This should be an action step that takes a little more time and commitment but will move the needle on your decision. You may think of 5-10 things that you can do in the next 30 days, and that is great! List them out and put the dates of when you plan to achieve them.

By putting together a legitimate action plan, you give yourself the clarity to know what it is going to take to make this change, and it starts to feel more real and possible. You can see yourself taking these simple steps to start and then tackling the harder ones as they come.

You've got to find that first step that is going to be comfortable for you to take. If you want to exercise more and you are not doing any exercise today, you can't jump right from no exercise to running a marathon. You have to find that first step that will help you get some movement but doesn't exhaust you so much that you refuse to do anything the next month. Maybe it's going on a twenty-minute walk to get started. Then, you can push it to a thirty-minute walk, and then you run a little, or you start doing some cardio in another form, but you've got to take the small steps. They still have to be challenging enough to find fulfillment. Sometimes a step in the right direction ends up being the most significant step of your life. Tiptoe if you must but take action.

Use the space below to write down what your action steps will be in the next 24 hours, the next week, and then over the next 30 days.

In the next 24 hours, I am going to:

____

____

____

In the next week, I am going to:

____

____

____

____

In the next 30 days, I am going to:

____

____

____

____

____

CHAPTER 9

Consistency

"It's not what we do once in a while that shapes our lives; it is what we do consistently."

—Tony Robbins

Every night my daughter has certain things that she likes before she goes to sleep. She wants a story read to her, and then she asks for a back massage and a foot rub. One night I said to her, you know I think you are a very lucky girl because I don't think every little girl is getting a back massage and a foot rub before they go to bed at night.

She looked up at me and said, "Mommy, that's because they don't ask."

I think I felt a hand slap me across the face as her words of wisdom hit me. If you want something, you have to ask and not just once but consistently ask for what you want.

She's not just consistent about asking for her nightly massage, but she is also very specific about what she likes and how she wants her massage. Even though we've been doing this for years, she still tells me exactly how she wants it done. She says, "mommy, start in the middle push down and then go out and work all the way up my back."

She is clear on what she wants, she's not afraid to ask for it, and she is consistent with her requests. She doesn't give up either. If we tell her no, she can't have a massage one night because it is too late or she has done something to lose that privilege, it doesn't stop her from asking the next night. She is persistent about going after what she wants. We can learn a lot from kids and their perseverance.

Creating Space for New

> *"Motivation is what gets you started. Habit is what keeps you going."*
>
> —Jim Rohn

We need to have those OMG moments in our lives. Those moments where we say, "I am going to do what?" Those moments when you decide you're going to do something big and bold. You don't know exactly how to do it yet, but you know you can.

Starting my business was one of those OMG moments for me. Getting paid to speak for the first time, having my first retreat, and several amazing trips with my husband have all been OMG moments. Writing this book has been another one of those moments.

I wasn't one of those people who said I have a book in me that I'm going to write someday. I did, however, want to be a speaker, so I joined a speaker's program. I had done a lot of speaking throughout my career, but I knew I still had a lot to learn to be more of a motivational speaker. I found a program where I could learn from two fantastic speakers and was ready to take my speaking to a new level. Then I found out that the yearlong program also included writing a book. The book was an afterthought in my mind. I was in the program to become a better speaker, not a writer. It all started to become real when I saw the deadlines and realized that I was way outside of my comfort zone.

I procrastinated and put it off for as long as I could. I didn't know the first thing about writing a book. But luckily, I was learning from a six-time New York Best Selling Author, Larry Winget. He gave me the tools, the process, and the push I needed to start putting words to paper finally.

At first, it was uncomfortable, but the more I researched, read books on my topic, and wrote, the more I started enjoying the process. After a while, I was excited. I couldn't wait to publish my book. I knew this was a message and a process that people needed to hear to help them make their big decisions and guide them through a lasting change.

I had to get out of my comfort zone and break some habits to start my business and to write this book. With each step that we take and each OMG moment we have, we have to make some shifts. Figure out what is serving us and what is not.

If you just live your life in your comfort zone, you will never have the OMG moments that excite you and scare you at the same time. Those are the moments we should live for, the ones that push us to become better and do more.

There are certain comfort zones or habits that serve us and others that don't. Brushing your teeth is an excellent habit to have. Whereas coming home every night and watching TV for hours is a comfort zone you may want to get out of if you're going to write a book, start a side hustle, spend more time with your family, or get in shape.

You have to evaluate the things you are regularly doing, break some of those habits, and get outside of your comfort zone when those things do not serve you.

When I was working full-time, getting my coaching certification, and starting my business, I had to give up some habits and prioritize other things in my life. I stopped watching TV and started getting up earlier to get some things done before I went into work.

I set aside Wednesday nights as my "school night" so that my kids knew that it was the night that I was working on my certification program. I would go straight from my job to my husband's office to do schoolwork. I had designated hours on the weekend that were times for me to work on my business and coach my clients. During the times that I set aside to build my business, I was so much more focused and was able to get things done faster.

I also made sure that I scheduled in family time and was more present during those times. Even though I had less time in my schedule, I felt like the time we did spend together was much more intentional, and I was not multitasking during those times.

When I was writing my book, I had to take a look at my schedule and habits again to see how to fit it in. I am more of a morning person, so I would spend at least thirty minutes in the morning, either reading books on my topic or writing. What I wrote wasn't always good or something that went into the book, it was more about creating the habit of doing it so that it became more natural and part of my routine.

Trying to multitask is just a distraction, and distractions can lower your performance and productivity by twenty percent. Don't think you can just multitask your way through it. You will be even less likely to achieve either thing when you do that.

If you want to create space for something new, you have to eliminate something. You can't just keep adding more and more to your plate without something coming off. Sometimes, it's stopping a bad habit, and other times it is deciding to give up one thing for another.

What bad habits do you need to stop doing to make a lasting change? How do you need to get outside of your comfort zone? What are some things you need to eliminate from your day to make space for your OMG moment?

____

____

____

____

____

____

What new, better habits do you need to create? What do you need to make room?

____

____

____

____

____

____

Schedule time for these new habits so that it is in your calendar, and you don't find yourself making excuses that you don't have time to do it. If you still can't find the time, then you still need to figure out what other habits or activities you need to give up to free up time for your new habit.

When it Never Seems to Work Out

"Our greatest weakness lies in giving up. The most certain way to succeed is always to try just one more time."

—Thomas A. Edison

I was working with someone who had recently married the love of her life, and she had just quit her job to build her business. Everything seemed to be going right in her life, and she was happier than she had been in a long time. But then she found herself about to sabotage it all.

She had run into an old coworker one day while she was out, and he started texting and calling her often. Then the conversations began to heat up, and he wanted more out of their relationship.

On our call, she opened up to me about what was going on, and she was perplexed about what to do. She found herself enjoying the attention and the conversations, but she said she knew that it wasn't the right thing to do. Yet she couldn't bring herself to end it with this guy.

As we discussed what was going on, it was apparent that she was self-sabotaging her marriage and her new business at the same time. All because she had an internal belief that she didn't deserve all this happiness and success.

For the first time, everything had been going right and as planned, and she didn't know how to handle that because that was not normal. When things in her life started going well, something would always happen to mess it up.

She was subconsciously looking for a way to screw things up because she didn't think she deserved a happy life. Once she realized what she was doing, and after we did some energy work to release this pattern in her life, she woke up the next morning completely clear on what she needed to do and ended the conversations with the old coworker.

It might seem like an easy decision looking on from the outside and when you're not the one in the situation. But when you have a pattern of self-sabotaging your success or have hit an upper limit, these decisions can be excruciating and so challenging to make.

For you, it might show up differently. Maybe you're picking fights with your spouse, your kids, parents, colleagues, or even friends. You may be eating food that you know isn't healthy instead of something that is going to give your body energy to sabotage your health. Or you might be spending money before you have it and getting further and further into debt.

Self-sabotage can come in many different forms, and at times you don't even realize that you are doing it to yourself. You don't realize that you have control over the situation and can choose differently to overcome it. It's a pattern where you enjoy a period of feeling outstanding and getting results, and then you do something to mess it up.

When you sabotage your decisions, it is a lot like pumping your brakes while driving. My grandfather used to drive this way. He had one foot on the gas and one foot on the brake. He would accelerate and then take his foot off the gas and then accelerate again and suddenly brake. I used to get so car sick riding with him.

This is what it feels like when you start getting some momentum in your life, and then you take your foot off the gas and lose speed. Then you hit the brakes and go spinning in a different direction that is not getting you anywhere near your goals.

You've got to learn to spot when you are taking your foot off the pedal or putting on the brakes for reasons that are sabotaging your progress and not because you need to.

Ask yourself:

- How am I getting in my way?
- Am I willing to have things in my life go well more often?
- Where am I stopping my progress?

Chasing after the Right Results

"When you're committed to something, you accept no excuses, only results."

—Ken Blanchard

When we go to the beach, my girls love to try and chase the birds. One bird lands on the ground and they go running after it until it flies away. Then another one lands, and they chase after that one. Of course, they never catch them, but they do get worn out and give up after a while.

Chasing after results can be a lot like chasing birds when you are not going after the right results, or you're not using the right tools. You use up a lot of energy going after something you want or are dreaming about, but when you get close to reaching it, it escapes you.

One year we rented a house down on the beach with a couple of other families. We were out on the beach hanging out after dinner, and one of the dads decided he was going to catch one of the birds that kept coming near us.

It was quite hilarious watching him plot out how to get close and dive in to try to catch the bird. It soon turned into a challenge that had the other dads betting whether he could do it. Then he caught one and for a few seconds held onto it. Don't worry; the bird was not hurt.

We did get a pretty funny picture out of it, but other than that... I'm not sure what the point was. He was covered in sand from head to toe from diving to capture the bird. It's not like he needed the bird, he wasn't going to do anything with it, and all it did was prove that he could catch a bird.

So many things you chase after leave you with the same results. You might make the ego proud of your rare accomplishment, but once the novelty wears off, you are still empty-handed, stuck cleaning up the mess it made, and no closer to anything that is going to get you a real result.

To get better results, first, you must focus on the real need. Stop chasing after things that seem nice to have or only play to the ego and get clear on your real need. Is your need to make enough money at your business so you can replace your corporate income? Is it to find a relationship where you are loved and appreciated and respect the other person?

Once you know what the real need is, understand all your options and think each option through. When you are clear on the best option, then the better results will come naturally.

Too many times, people chase after the things they want before the things they need. Things they want, give them a quick satisfaction whereas things they need can take longer, and can be more challenging to achieve.

A want is a wish. A need is a necessity.

When you face a decision, ask yourself, is this something I need, or just something I want?

You have to start prioritizing your needs and wants. When you've done what you need to do, you can start doing what you want. But make the decisions and the goals based on your needs first.

Bishop T.D. Jakes said, "*Stop watering things that were never meant to grow in your life. Water what works, what's good, what's right... Stop wasting water on dead issues, dead relationships, dead people, a dead past. No matter how much you water concrete, you can't grow a garden.*"

Stop wasting your energy on things that aren't working or not getting you the results that you need. You only have so much energy, so you need to focus on what is going to get you the right results.

Where are you chasing after the wrong results? Where have you set a goal that is ego-based but doesn't deliver any real results? Where are you putting your wants before your real needs? Where are you watering dead plants?

____

____

____

____

____

____

When you can recognize where you're focusing or doing the wrong things, only then can you get the right answers and start doing what really will work.

How can you turn these around and start chasing after the right results? What are the real plants in your life that you need to be watering? What is the real need that you need to fulfill?

____

____

____

____

____

____

Building Momentum

> *"There will be obstacles. There will be doubters. There will be mistakes. But with hard work, there are no limits."*
>
> —Michael Phelps

When you start chasing after the right results, you will see what is working and what isn't working. But you first have to try. You will never know what will work if you don't try anything. Figure out what works for you and start doing more of what works and less of what doesn't work.

When you make a decision that produces the right result, you should do more of that. When you start to do more of that all day and in every situation, then you build up a consistent pattern of behavior that creates the result that you want.

The more you do it, the easier it gets. If you do something once, you're going to still fall back into your same patterns. You have to be consistent for it to become more natural. If you want to lose weight, you can't just go out and eat healthy once. You've got to create that consistency, create the momentum to build it up to make it to the point where it just becomes natural.

There's a term called muscle memory. You want the consistency of behavior to become like muscle memory, where you do not even have to think so much. You're just doing the right thing because you've proven to yourself that it creates the right result. You want to get to the point that you don't have to question anymore if it is the right decision. You just know that it is going to give you the results you desire, so you do it.

Let's face it, the first time you do anything, it isn't going to go perfectly. Sometimes it might even be a disaster. You can't just do it once and expect to be a master, that requires practice and consistently showing up to try again.

I remember the first time I did a Facebook live. I had no idea what I was doing. I thought, who is even going to watch this? It was uncomfortable, I stumbled over my words, I didn't have a message, and I wanted to hit delete when I got done. The next time it got a little easier, but it wasn't until I started doing them consistently for a month that I finally started to feel more comfortable and build some momentum.

If you give up after a fumbled attempt to do something, you will never get to your goal. You've got to push through the awkward stage until you create that muscle memory that makes it easier and will build momentum.

Basketball players do not make it to the NBA unless they are consistent with their practice and are committed. When they first started, they were probably lucky if they made a couple of baskets. But when they did make one, the excitement was intense, and it gave them the desire to do it again and again.

If they were to evaluate their progress based on the percentage of baskets made when they first started playing, they would have given up years ago. But they understand that they will never reach 100% accuracy, and that is okay. It's about pushing harder and harder to get better results and not giving up.

When you're talking to your kids, you've got to be consistent. When the Coronavirus hit, and we were quarantined, my girls were in first and third grade. The first day I sat down to do remote learning with them, I was trying to do my work at the same time. I would give them a task and then start to email a client or have to get on a call. I quickly realized that it wasn't working. They would get distracted and want to play or just goof off and not finish their school work.

By that afternoon, I quickly realized that we had to make a change. They needed me to be focused for them to be focused. They required me to be consistent with my directions. I had to change how my days were structured. I moved all my clients to the afternoons and freed up my mornings to be dedicated entirely to them.

When I gave them my full attention, they got things done faster, and their excitement for remote learning started to build. I had to consistently show up for them in the right frame of mind. It gave me a new respect for teachers and how they have to show up each day and the consistency they have to provide to our kids so that the kids can build their learning momentum.

When my daughter was first starting to learn math, I asked her what two plus two was, and she said five. If I had given up on her and said, "math just isn't her thing," she would have never learned that it is four.

It's no big deal to have to work with a child to help them learn some of those basic skills. They do the problems over and over and get the flashcards to test them to build that muscle memory. You don't let them give up after a couple of tries. They have to keep trying until they get it right.

Let's say you're a business manager, and you know you need to hire someone. You go through the process of creating the job description, interviewing candidates, and finally hiring someone. They seemed like the perfect candidate and said all the right things during the interview. After a few months, you realize that they are so bad at the job and not the right fit for the position. And now you've got to get rid of them.

It doesn't mean that you never hire anybody ever again. You don't just sit there with no employee to do the job. You have to keep hiring. You'll get better the next time, you'll ask different questions, and you'll have different standards because you know more.

You don't give up just because you had a little setback. You figure out what didn't go well, what you need to adjust, and you try again. Each time you learn something new, and you get better and better at it as it becomes easier and more manageable. And when you get it right, the results are exhilarating.

You start to build momentum when you start having successes. Then the achievements start to get closer and closer together, and the momentum picks up and drives even more success.

In the Clarity Trifecta, consistency is the circle around the triangle that helps you keep moving. It's like when you are building a snowball, and you start with a small pack of snow in your hands. That's the small amount of clarity, confidence, courage, and commitment you have when you first start out making a change. The more you roll that snowball in the snow, the bigger and bigger it gets. Rolling the snowball is you being consistent.

The first push you give gives you a little more clarity. Then you give it another push and get some confidence. Keep pushing, and you find the courage to take action. The commitment starts to build as you now have a goal to make this snowball so big because it has a specific meaning to you that will drive you. When your snowball gets to a certain size, it starts to get easier to push, and you realize it's not taking as much effort to push it forward as long as you keep it moving.

However, if you stop, it becomes even harder to start up again. You've lost the momentum, and the snow has started to lose its form on the bottom and become flat. To get the snowball moving again, it takes a bigger push. You don't have to start completely over, but you have to find the muscle and drive to make those initial pushes to get it moving again.

The same is true with your change. If you stop for a while and let the momentum die, it is going to take a big push to get you moving again, and you will not get back to that place where it was easy for a while. You don't just pick back up where you left off and keep going at the same speed.

When you look at where you haven't been consistent, what shows up for you? Where do you see yourself starting and then stopping and then trying to start again? How has this impacted your progress? Journal about where you lack consistency in your life right now.

____

____

____

____

____

____

Let's start building your momentum so that you can reach that goal. What three things can you start doing every day to be more consistent? Three action steps that will start to build momentum to help you reach your goal. Schedule these into your day.

Being consistent in the morning is a great way to start your day. Do you have a morning routine? Mine changes over time as I try new things, and as I'm at different phases of life. One thing that I have done for the last year consistently is a quick meditation when I first wake up. It's one I created called the "Shower of Blessings."

A year ago, I was having one of those days where everything was just going right. I won a big prize worth over two thousand dollars at an event, I signed a new client, and I got asked to speak at an event that excited me. Everything that day was just falling into place.

As I got off the phone with the new clients, the excitement overwhelmed me. I felt chills throughout my body. Then I heard it raining outside, and the chills started to feel like raindrops on my body. I started to think about each one of those raindrops as a blessing in my life. I was thinking about the day I had just had and the wins that I had over the last week, and then I started to think about the incredible blessings in my life over the previous month, year, and throughout my life.

As I thought about each one, I visualized them raining down on me like a blessing. Each one hit my skin, and I could feel it. I anchored in that feeling of each blessing, and it was like a flood started pouring down on me.

Every morning when I wake up, I take my Shower of Blessings while I'm still lying in bed. I think about the blessings already in my life, and I feel each one hitting me like a raindrop. Then I ask myself, what blessings do I want to show up today? What do I need this week? And I start to feel those blessings coming into my life and touching me like raindrops.

This is how I start my day, and it puts me in a place of feeling blessed but also knowing that I have so much more coming to me. It gets me focused on what I need to do to make those blessings come into my life.

Another thing I do every day is I have a reminder set on my phone that pops up with a mantra. I change it every so often as I see a negative self-talk pop up or realize that I've been getting in my own way and need to reframe something. The one I have right now pops up at nine o'clock every morning and says, "I expand in abundance, success, and love every day, as I inspire those around me to do the same."

You can take one or two of the positive affirmations you wrote down in Chapter 6 and plug that into your phone as a reminder to say it to yourself consistently.

I'm consistent about telling my kids and my husband every day that I love them. Finding time within the day to snuggle with my girls is always a priority. Having time to have a real conversation with my husband every day is one way that I try to ensure we are on the same page, and we find time to listen to each other.

I also consistently take action in my business every day. The activity varies depending on what I am focused on at that time, but I always try to make sure that I do at least one income-generating activity every day. That might be following up with leads, reaching out for speaking gigs, doing a speaking event, or a Facebook live or going to a networking event. It's about consistently making an effort to show up in my business and do things that will help me grow instead of things that are just distractions.

I consistently have my tea every morning. Oh wait, that's probably not getting me to my goals. Just a habit. Ha-ha!

So, what are the three things that you are going to start consistently doing every day that will make a difference in creating your lasting change? Write them down below and put them into your calendar, so they happen.

____

____

____

____

____

____

CHAPTER 10

Commitment

> *"Some succeed because they are destined to, but most succeed because they are determined to."*
>
> —Henry Van Dyke

I've left commitment for last because here's the challenge: It ends with commitment, but it also starts with commitment. It begins with a commitment to yourself to start going after what you've said you wanted. It starts with a commitment that you are now willing to make new decisions, to create new actions that will get you new results.

We started this book talking about how everything you're experiencing in your life; is a result of the decisions you've made. You made those decisions. Why don't you, right now, become committed to making a new decision?

I know in my life, it's much easier to become committed to making a decision that gets me the result that I want, so I don't have to be stuck with the choices of the past.

"I will try" is not a commitment. Just do it or do not do it.

Commitment is the foundation. It is where it all begins and ends.

By this time, you should have a pretty clear picture of what it is going to take to make a change if you've been doing the work along the way as you read this book. You should understand where some of your most significant setbacks have come from, what your biggest obstacles to overcome are, and where you've been chasing after the wrong results.

Are you ready to face those things? Or are you going to decide you are comfortable where you are?

You may realize throughout this book that you need to get help. There might be areas you find yourself getting stuck in and can't move forward. Invest in yourself and get the help you need. You deserve it. When you invest in yourself, you're telling the universe that you mean business. Invest both time and money in yourself.

Time and money are also the biggest excuses that keep people in their comfort zone. People aren't willing to take the time it takes to make a lasting change or spend money on something that is going to help them through that. That just means it isn't a priority to you right now. Maybe someday it will be, but hopefully, that is before it is too late, or someone forces you to make the decision.

The Wakeup Call

> *"In the absence of wakeup calls, many of us never really confront the critical issues of life."*
>
> —Stephen Covey

I got a phone call from a friend when I was on my way home from work. Usually, these calls are our way of catching up every month or two as we live in different states, and both have little kids that keep us busy, so we don't get to talk as often as we used to. She's someone who always made me laugh, and we joked about silly things from high school and how she was still trying to figure out what she wanted to do with the rest of her life even though she was already in her thirties. She had switched from one career to another and never quite landed in a job that lit her up, other than her hobby of photography. We had recently talked about how she should just go for it and start a photography business.

But this call was not our usual banter. I could hear in her voice that something was not right. She went on to tell me that she had just found out that she had breast cancer.

I gulped back tears as I wasn't sure how to respond. My heart sank, and all I could think was how could this be? She was healthy with two young kids. My mind started spinning and wondering what the treatment would be and how I could help and support her.

Then a few weeks later, I got an email from someone I used to work with, telling me that my old boss was diagnosed with breast cancer. I sank into my couch, closed my eyes, and thought, why? She was such a strong and ambitious woman with a young daughter.

About a month later, I got another call from an old colleague telling me that one of my other friends had also been diagnosed with breast cancer.

Over the next year, I had six friends and former colleagues get diagnosed with breast cancer. It was like there was no end. I started to wonder who was going to be next, afraid to answer the phone as there seemed to be something in the water that year.

They all started their journey to fight it. And after a long battle for each of them, they all came out of it and went into remission, each with their methods of treatment and some that went on longer than others. I was so grateful for the healing and that they all came through it. There was a feeling that we could breathe again.

Then a couple of years later, one after the other over a few months, I found out that for three of them, cancer had come back. This time it was spreading fast.

The news that one of my friends was being taken to Hospice for her last days led to a hard conversation with her as she tried to be positive through it all for her son. Attending her funeral felt surreal. She was only in her mid-thirties. She was too young to die.

Then six months later, my other friend took a turn for the worse. She lived three hours from any close friends or family and needed help as her husband was a pilot, so he would be gone for days at a time. Four of us that went to high school with her decided we would each take a week and stay with her. We were flying in from all over the US, and we all wanted to help her and be there for her.

I was designated to be there the second week. I don't think I realized how bad my friend was until I got there. She always had the most gorgeous, long, red hair that I had ever seen. To see her without it and skinnier than ever was disheartening.

I cherished that week with her and her two kids. She never lost hope even though she faced some really tough decisions, like whether or not to let them drill a hole in her head. I can't even imagine what she went through.

It was hard to leave after that week, but I also wanted to get home to my two babies and hug them and never let them go.

One week after I left, she passed away.

Her passing was my wakeup call!

This was the moment that I said, "I have to figure out a better way to live my life."

I had to stop, take a step back, and look at my life from a new perspective. How did I want to live the rest of my life? What did I need to change? This wakeup call lit a fire under my butt to start living for today and stop waiting for tomorrow. It gave me the drive to want more. It woke me up to realize that there is more to life than working sixty hours a week for someone else.

I wanted more time with my kids and my husband. I wanted to have more freedom and flexibility. I was tired of living by someone else's rules. This was when I decided to become a coach.

I suddenly had a burning desire to help others that felt stuck in their jobs too, or those like my friend, who could never quite figure out what they wanted to be when they grew up.

This was the turning point for me.

Your wakeup call may look different than mine. It can come in many forms and at the most surprising times. It's doesn't always have to be a death or some major catastrophe.

For one of my friends, her wakeup call was when she realized she could barely get up the six steps from her garage to her house because her knee hurt so bad. She picked up the call and lost fifty pounds.

For many people, 9/11 was a big wakeup call. For others, COVID-19 made them re-evaluate their priorities and their relationships. I mean, you get quarantined in the house with a spouse that you barely talk to anymore, and something is bound to shift one way or the other.

What is the wakeup call that you have gotten? What are you doing to reprioritize and figure out your brighter future?

I have to admit, even I need to remind myself at times of that year that I lost three friends. The year that I decided things had to change. Writing this now makes me think, have I done enough? What else can I do to live an even better life? The losses of that year are my anchor that pulls me back down to reality when I start drifting away. It is my reminder that life is not predictable or a given. This is where I find my drive to commit to lasting change.

There's a realization moment, where you say enough is enough. A place where you realize that your heart isn't full. A situation that leaves you stunned and speechless.

You may have walked into your office one day and been told you were fired. Or you came home, and your spouse said it's over.

Where do you find your drive? What is your wakeup call trying to tell you? Reflect on what has happened or is happening to you now that is the wakeup call you need to drive a decision for change. Write it down here.

____

____

____

____

____

____

Knowing Your Why

> *"It doesn't matter where you're coming from. All that matters is where you want to go, how you're going to get there, and attaching your why to make sure you go out there and accomplish it!"*
>
> —Dean Graziosi

When I decided that I wanted to go into coaching and start my own business, one of my drivers was that I was just ready to get away from some of the politics in the corporate world. I was ready for a new chapter in my life.

But that was just a surface driver. Surface drivers are a reason that will get you to a point and might excite you enough to work hard for the change that you want. They are great for hitting some of the smaller midpoint goals, like losing ten pounds to fit into a dress for a wedding or saving enough to buy a new house.

These are important to know and have, but if you find yourself getting to that point and then slipping right back to where you were or not getting the results you want, it is typically because you are missing your bigger why.

To make a lasting change, you've got to know what your why is that will keep you motivated and committed for the long haul. What's the underlying reason that this change is so important to you? Why is this change going to make a difference in your life? Why does this need to be a lasting change? And not something that you just dabble at for a minute, or that you take a stab at, and if it doesn't work out, you give up.

Until you know what the underlying why is, you don't fully commit. It's like we're halfway in and halfway out. We think we want something, but we don't know exactly why we want it, or what it's going to do for us. Then it's just not going to happen. So, you've got to get clear on what it is you want and why you want it.

My bigger why involved finding freedom in my life and showing my girls that you don't have to settle. I wanted to have freedom, and that was huge for me. I also wanted to have flexibility in my life so that I could run out at three o'clock and get my girls if I need to. I wanted to show my girls that they can have what they want in life if they go after it. And I wanted to be an influencer and inspire other people to know that they can do the same. That is the why that has been driving me in the last few years.

You want to figure out what will drive you to completely commit and not give up along the way regardless of how hard things get. It's going to be different for each person. Everybody has a different reason for why they want something.

It is what will drive you forward, keep you on track and keep you consistent so that you don't sway. It will encourage you to find the right answers when you need them when you think about why you will not give up.

So, you need to establish what your driving forces are behind this change. Why is this so important to you? Why is this going to make such an impact on your life? Why do you want to change? And it's typically not the first thing that comes to your mind or your surface level answer. There is usually something underneath that surface that is going to help drive you even further.

A woman reached out to me after seeing some advice I gave to someone else in a group. She had a desire to start a coaching business but was struggling to figure out what the business should be. As we were talking, she said "I had a coach tell me I need to figure out my Why, but I'm struggling to understand what that is."

I said, "Yes, knowing your why is important, so let's figure that out now."

I asked her, "Why is it important to you to be a successful coach?"

She responded, "Because I am a single mom of three kids, and I want a better life for my kids."

I then asked, "Why is it important for you to have a better life for your kids?"

She said, "They deserve to have a better future. My parents gave me everything I needed, and I want my kids to have that. I want to give them the best shot at life."

Then I asked her, "Why is it important for you to give them the best shot at life?"

She paused, and tears started to come to her eyes. Then she said, "They deserve that. Everyone deserves that. Everyone has the potential to succeed, but not everyone is given the same opportunities."

She went on to tell me how she had been through things in her life that made her give up, how she had overcome some incredible things to get to where she was. She wanted her kids and everyone else to know that they have opportunities, and they can change things and overcome their situation. Sharing this and helping people through those difficult times was what got to the soul of her why. It was to show her kids and others the opportunities to succeed so that they could live to their fullest potential and she could as well.

This is what will drive her to show up for those people who need her. When she thinks about her kids and the opportunities that she wants to give them, it will keep her pushing forward to build her business and be successful.

Now it is your turn to figure out your Why. When I ask you why you want to make this decision or change, what is the first thing that comes to your mind? What is the very first thing that comes to your mind when I ask why you want to be successful in making this change? It might be that you're in a relationship where you're arguing all the time, and you want to have more peace in your relationships. Maybe it's because you have a boss who you don't get along with or who doesn't respect you, and you want to be recognized for what you do. Maybe your kids are going off to college, and now you're wondering, what do I do, how do I find fulfillment in my life when there's a gap.

Whatever the change is that you are going through the decision with which you are struggling. I want you to think about why you want to make it and be successful. Write it down below.

Level 1: I want to be successful with this change because

____

____

Your first response is probably more of a surface level answer unless you've already done some of this work before. As you continue to ask yourself these questions, you will get deeper into the real reason why it is so crucial.

It's typically around the third or the fourth time, where you start to see a real shift in your responses. You start to feel it hit you in the gut, and you realize that you're getting closer. When you feel that go another level deep and see if there's an even deeper level to your why. You usually hit your deep, big why between levels five and seven of asking yourself why.

So, I want you to try this with the situation you're in, with something that you want to change the impact that you want to have in, or why you want to be successful in your life and business. If you have someone you can do this with, it helps to ask each other the questions.

As you ask yourself the second time, you are going to fill in your question with the response you gave for the first question. For example, when I asked the women earlier the first time why it was important to her to be successful, her response was "because I want a better life for my kids." So the next level was to ask, "Why is it important for you to have a better life for your kids?"

Take the answer you wrote down when I asked you the first time why it was important to you. Keep doing this until you feel you've hit it and then ask yourself one more time to see if there is an even deeper level.

Level 2: Why is it important to you to (fill in with answer from Level 1)

____

____

Answer: __________________________________

____

Level 3: Why is it important to you to (fill in with answer from Level 2)

____

____

Answer: ____

____

Level 4: Why is it important to you to (fill in with answer from Level 3)

____

____

Answer: ____

____

Level 5: Why is it important to you to (fill in with answer from Level 4)

____

Answer: ____

____

Level 6: Why is it important to you to (fill in with answer from Level 5)

____

Answer: ____

____

Level 7: Why is it important to you to (fill in with answer from Level 6)

____

Answer: ____

____

Commit To Yourself

"The major value in life is not what you get. The major in life is what you become."

—Jim Rohn

I believe life is a gift. We have so much time to do with it whatever we decide to do. You can decide to sit back on the sidelines and stay off the radar so that no one knows who you are. You can be afraid to step out and do anything different. Or you can commit to standing up and making a difference. You can commit to making a change. You can commit to making the rest of your life even better. You can commit to contributing. You can commit to whatever it is that you desire to do, but you haven't yet in your life.

You can desire something, but that is not enough. Desire is not enough to keep you focused and keep you moving forward. You have to have the motivation and commitment to actually make it happen.

There are too many people who say they want something, but the reality is they aren't willing to do what it takes. Are you willing to do what it takes? Are you willing to take the steps? Are you willing to take action to make it happen?

When you fully commit to something, and you say that you are willing to stand for it, the universe responds and will start shifting to line things up to help you make it happen. If you're not quite sure if you're fully committed, or there is any hesitation, the universe will challenge you. It tests you to see just how committed you are.

The quote above from Jim Rohn talks about how setting the goal was more about who we become on the path to meeting that goal than actually reaching the goal.

So, if you're not even trying. If you're not even making an effort to make some sort of change in an area where you're feeling stressed, unhappy, unsatisfied, or unsure, then you're not going to change, and you're going to stay the same.

The choice is up to you. You get to decide.

But if you decide you want to make a change, then you've also got to decide to commit to it 100%. Commit to getting the clarity you need to find the right path. Commit to getting the confidence and courage you need to drive forward. Commit to showing up consistently to build momentum and create a lasting change.

You've gotten this far in the book, so I know you are committed to at least reading this book. I give you credit for making it this far.

But did you do the work along the way? Did you put the work in to get the clarity you need to make the best decision for you? Did you determine what your brighter future looks like and develop your plan to get to it? What is your reason for wanting to achieve that one goal? What's your driver?

If you did, then you have already seen some clarity in your life. You've seen what could be possible if you commit to making it happen. You've seen the negative self-talk that is holding you back and are probably already starting to see some results of replacing them with positive affirmations. If you've been doing the work along the way, then you've already taken at least one of your first steps. Congratulations!

This is your time to commit fully to being better, to doing the work, to not giving up, and to making the decision that will bring you the lasting change you truly desire.

Put it in writing to solidify your commitment.

I, (insert name) ________________________________ commit to making the decision to (insert your decision) ________________ ____, in order to change my life (in this way) ________________________________ ____.

Signed: ____

Date: __________________________

CHAPTER 11

Live With Your Decision

"Until a person can say deeply and honestly, 'I am what I am today because of the choices I made yesterday.' That person cannot say, 'I choose otherwise.'"

—Steven Covey

Do you now see how everything in your life is the result of the decisions you've made? It's not always an easy pill to swallow that we are where we are because of our own decisions. You can either decide now to make a new decision or live with the choices you've made.

If you decide to make a new decision, I've given you the tools to figure out the best decision for you. You now recognize that it's time to stop avoiding the decision and ignoring the signs that are trying to wave

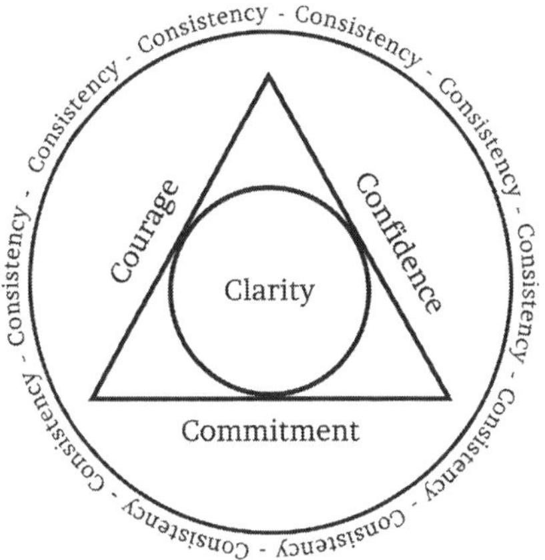

you in a new direction. You have the Clarity Trifecta formula to help you make a lasting change.

Start by getting clarity around what your brighter future looks and visualizing what that looks like for you. What is different? What do you want to achieve? Then, figure out the specific and measurable goals you need to set to help you achieve that brighter future.

As you start to get clarity around your decision, your confidence will start to grow. Your faith and belief that you can make this change will start to set in. Remember what the greatest version of you is and continue working on eliminating the negative self-talk that sets you back. As you go throughout your days, recognize your physical state and use movement, music, or the brush off to improve your physical state.

Surround yourself with certainty by finding the right people to have in your life as coaches, mentors, accountability partners and even as friends. Seek out those that will help you through this change, support you, and push you to be better.

Celebrate every little accomplishment you have along your journey towards your lasting change. Recognize when you said no when you would have said yes before, and it kept you on track to meet your goal. Rejoice when you achieve even just the small steps on your way to your goal.

Each one of those steps takes courage. The courage to let go of the story you've been holding onto or the excuses you've been telling yourself about why you couldn't make a change. The courage to take ownership of those and recognize that there might be a reason this has happed for you and not to you.

The courage to stop waiting on someone else or for something else to happen first. The courage to make the decision. The courage to move forward with your life, take that first step and make it better than it is today.

You cannot make a lasting change without consistency. You will have to let go of bad habits and get out of your comfort zone to make room for new habits that will help you be more consistent and build your momentum. Notice when you start to stall or ruin your progress and what it is that is getting in your way. Recognize how you are sabotaging your results and adjust to do more of what is working for you.

Make sure you are chasing after the right results that are going to actually get you to your goal and are not just a distraction or playing to your ego. Then start building your momentum by putting in place you daily routine. Have at least 3 things you do every day that create a habit and start getting you closer to achieving your goal.

The foundation and where it starts and ends is commitment. You have to be committed to making this change. Sometimes, it takes that wake-up call for us to be shaken out of our lives' monotony to realize that a change is needed. To fully commit to something, you have to understand why. Your why will drive you to move forward when you want to give up.

Commit to developing your next steps and getting the information and the help that you need to make this a lasting change. It takes a lot of self-control and energy to make a lasting change. These are, however, exhaustible resources. It's like when you're lifting weights; at first, it's relatively easy, and then your muscles start to get tired. The more weight you lift, the harder it gets. The more significant the change you're going to make, the more it will take a toll on your self-control.

Change is hard because people wear themselves out. What looks like laziness is often exhaustion. So you need to make sure that you are not wearing yourself out and give yourself downtime. But it's also critical to make sure you are challenged enough to make it appealing to change.

I've laid out for you how to make a better decision and the formula to create a lasting change. It's up to you to decide if you're going to use it. If you do apply these concepts, your life could be dramatically different. You deserve to make a lasting change. You can commit to it right now or go back to how everything has been.

If you don't decide to make a change, you need to accept the way it is. Stop complaining about it, stop saying it isn't your fault and stop pretending there isn't anything you can do about it. If you get nothing else out of this book, please walk away taking ownership of where you are in your life and recognizing that your decisions got you to exactly where you are.

You have complete control to choose how you move forward. You have the choice to decide how you are going to react to things that might be out of your control.

Life is hard! Life is unpredictable! No one ever promised you that it would be fair. You can decide to live in a place of resentment and anger or decide to do something to make the most of it.

You can look at where you are right now and decide to make a change. Decide that you are not satisfied with the status quo. Decide that it isn't okay to settle. Decide that you do have a brighter future. Decide to get help and support. Decide to feel differently.

I know that this isn't the first book you've read, and you've probably heard a lot of the things in this book before in different ways. But there is a reason that you are here reading this now. There is something you are meant to get out of it this time. Decision making is a muscle, and you may need to go back and reread parts of this book to master those areas.

Are you going to apply what you've learned here and start making better decisions? Or are you going to put it back on the shelf and let it collect dust?

Please do something, anything. Make even a small decision that moves you closer to where you want to go. Any decision is better than no decision.

ACKNOWLEDGMENTS

It makes me humbled and appreciative to be able to acknowledge so many people in my life that have influenced this book and my life.

I have to start by thanking my husband, Glenn Jaffe, who has always been my biggest supporter. He even proofread this book while I was in surgery so that I could meet my publishing deadline. He has been my sounding board throughout and knows when I need a little pick me up.

Thank you to Suzanne Evans and Larry Winget, who have been my book and speaking coaches that have pushed me to go after my goals. Their candid feedback has made me a better author, speaker and coach.

Thank you to my book accountability group, Lauren Crigler, Janet Ickes, Laurie Johnson, Michele Maddox, and Lauren McClerkin, who were the best book mastermind partners. In order to get myself to sit down and write, I knew I needed to surround myself with others doing the same thing, and we all pushed and supported each other through the process of getting our books out of us.

Thank you to my mom, Janice Hammer, who has always taught me to never give up. Thank you to my dad, Royce Hammer, who taught me the value of hard work and staying committed. Having them both here locally watching our girls and helping them grow up to be incredible young ladies is a blessing.

Thank you to all my current and previous mastermind partners and business besties that have inspired me, and encouraged me along this entrepreneurial journey. Juli Gauthier, Lori Granito, Cassandra Shepard, Kathy Haan, Mia LaMotte, Lynne Roe, Pat Delgado, and

Danette Alexandra Malcolm, you have each impacted my life and the decisions I have made for the better.

I have been blessed with so many amazing friends, too many to name here, that have supported me and checked in on me throughout my life. Thank you all!

I want to thank those who challenged me, disagreed with me, and didn't believe in me. I would not be where I am without your actions pushing me to be better and to do more with my life. I recognize that you did these things for me and not to me, regardless of what your intentions were.

I look forward to the new people I will connect with because of this book and the relationships it will form.

ABOUT THE AUTHOR

Tami Jaffe is a mom of two girls, Teagan and Cora, and wife to chiropractor, Dr. Glenn Jaffe. Their family has a love of travel, massages, and snuggling.

Tami is a career transition and business success coach, energy shifter, author, and speaker who inspires successful professionals who dream of resigning and doing something new. Tami helps guide her clients through the sometimes overwhelming prospect of changing careers or starting a new business.

Tami has over 20 years of leadership experience with companies ranging from startups to mid-size to Fortune 100 companies so she knows what it takes in any size organization to be a successful leader. She is committed to helping others make the best decisions so that they can find the success they want in their life, businesses and careers.

Tami offers a wide range of coaching services and programs. Her inspiring retreats, individual coaching, online courses, workshops, masterminds, and keynote speeches support professionals in reaching their highest visions by getting clarity on their future and developing the courage and confidence to claim a better life.

As the founder of Tami Jaffe Coaching, Tami has spoken at conferences and events around the world. If you're looking for a speaker for your next event or need a success coach, reach out to Tami through her website www.tamijaffe.com.

Made in the USA
Middletown, DE
01 October 2021

49032537R00088